THE WORLD'S MOST POWERFUL

HANDGUNS AND RIFLES

THE WORLD'S MOST POWERFUL

HANDGUNS AND RIFLES

ROBERT ADAM

JG PRESS

A QUINTET BOOK

Published in the USA 1996 by JG Press.
Distributed by World Publications, Inc.

The JG Press imprint is a trademark of
JG Press, Inc.
455 Somerset Avenue
North Dighton, MA 02764

This edition produced for sale in the USA, its
territories and dependencies only.

ISBN 1-57215-176-5

This book was designed and produced by
Quintet Publishing Limited
6 Blundell Street
London N7 9BH

Creative Director: Terry Jeavons
Designer: Stuart Walden
Project Editors: Caroline Beattie, Damian Thompson
Editor: Ann Cree
Illustrator: Danny McBride
Photographer: Paul Forrester

Typeset in Great Britain by
Central Southern Typesetters, Eastbourne
Manufactured in Hong Kong by
Regent Publishing Services Limited
Printed in Singapore by
Star Standard Industries (Pte) Ltd.

DEDICATION

This book is dedicated to gunmakers and
shooters the world over. Without the skill
of the gunmaker, none of the firearms
illustrated herein would have been
produced, nor would they function so well.
Without the needs of the shooter to fulfil,
new calibres and types of ammunition
would not have been made. Their
partnership has resulted in a creativity and
inventiveness almost unrivalled in any
other field. Long may it continue.

ROB ADAM

1991

CONTENTS

1

THE QUEST FOR POWER

OWER TENDS TO CORRUPT AND ABSOLUTE POWER COR-
rupts absolutely.' When Lord Acton penned his now
famous quotation in 1887, he was thinking of political authority. In the history of the world, political power has often
grown from the barrels of guns. By possessing more and
bigger firearms, absolute firepower has given many politi-
cians absolute national, and more recently, global, authority.

For many years, the quest for power through rifles and
handguns was driven by the consumable needs of warring
governments. The advent of nuclear weapons gave them an
alternative and vastly destructive capability. As a result of
the so-called Nuclear Umbrella, military smallarms development has concentrated on small calibre, high capacity
firearms with 'adequate' rather than absolute firepower. It
has been left to sports people and firearms enthusiasts to
develop more powerful hand- and shoulder-fired pieces in
the second half of the 20th century.

THE BEGINNING

Firearms designs are many and diverse. However, they all
share one common feature, in that they burn a propellant in
a closed chamber. This burning is exceedingly rapid and
generates large quantities of hot gas. The gas pressure is
contained behind a projectile, usually a bullet, which blocks
the only way out of the chamber. When the pressure generated by the burning propellant is sufficiently high, the bullet
is driven out of the chamber and down the gun's barrel.

The first propellant used was gunpowder, now more commonly known as black powder. The explosive and propellant
capability of black powder has been known since before
the 14th century. It is widely accepted that the definitive
recipe for gunpowder was recorded around 1320 by Berthold
Schwartz, a monk living in Freiburg, Germany. Although the
true origins of the propellant are unrecorded, the effect of
various forms of saltpetre-based gunpowders have been
noted since at least 275.

Black powder is made from a ground-up mechanical
mixture of 75% saltpetre (potassium nitrate), 15% charcoal
and 10% sulphur, and the purity of the ingredients used
determines how easily it ignites and the amount of gas it can
generate. Early mixtures ignited erratically and armies were
forced to rely heavily on swords and bows instead of their
slow, ponderous cannon, or primitive 'hand gonnes'. A dis-
advantage of black powder as a propellant is that it actually
burns slowly in modern terms, generating only moderate
pressures and leaving behind substantial corrosive residues.
To gain the maximum effect from black powder, large bore
guns which fired very heavy projectiles were made. The
velocities of these projectiles are now considered quite
sedate, from 500 to 800 fps (150 to 250 mps), but the velocity
combined with the weight still gave the projectile substantial
'muzzle energy' and destructive power.

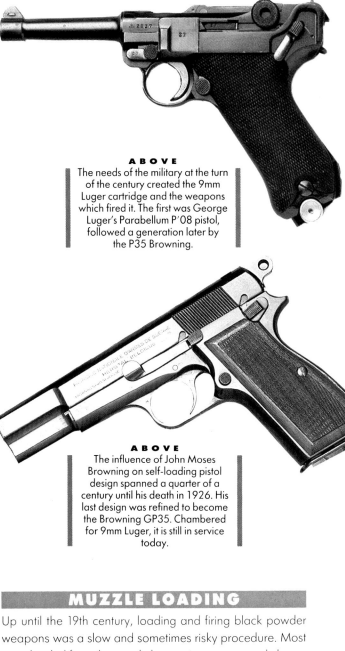

ABOVE
The needs of the military at the turn
of the century created the 9mm
Luger cartridge and the weapons
which fired it. The first was George
Luger's Parabellum P'08 pistol,
followed a generation later by
the P35 Browning.

ABOVE
The influence of John Moses
Browning on self-loading pistol
design spanned a quarter of a
century until his death in 1926. His
last design was refined to become
the Browning GP35. Chambered
for 9mm Luger, it is still in service
today.

MUZZLE LOADING

Up until the 19th century, loading and firing black powder
weapons was a slow and sometimes risky procedure. Most
were loaded from the muzzle by pouring a measured charge
of propellant down into the barrel, on top of which was
rammed wadding to help seal in pressure, followed by a
bullet or ball. Ignition of the powder was through a small
hole known as a flash hole or touch hole at the closed
breech end; it was accomplished by a spark from a flint in
the most popular smallarms, or from a slow match for
cannon. The dangers were that traces of still-glowing
powder from a previous shot could set off the next charge
before it was rammed or aimed, and flint ignition could be
upset by inclement weather.

PERCUSSION CAPS

Firearms technology changed rapidly in the 19th century.
The first significant development was in the use of metal
fulminate compounds as detonators for gunpowder. The

explosive properties of small quantities of fulminates had been known since the beginning of the 18th century, but it was a Scottish clergyman, Alexander Forsyth, who first applied for a patent in 1807 to use them for firing weapons by striking a fulminate pill at the flash hole. Forsyth's patent was soon modified by others so that the fulminate priming compound was enclosed in a soft metal cup which fitted over a hollow nipple behind the main charge. When hit by a spring-powered hammer, the fulminate would generate sufficient flash to reliably ignite a powder charge in a muzzle-loaded pistol or rifle. Indeed, Colonel Samuel Colt used percussion caps on the six chambers of his .44 calibre Walker Colt revolver, a very powerful 6-shot handgun designed for Texas Ranger Captain S H Walker in 1847. Walker wanted a repeating sidearm that could be carried on horseback, not on his hip. Colt modified his small Paterson revolver design and came up with one of the largest and most powerful black powder revolvers ever made.

METALLIC RIMFIRE CARTRIDGES

The next great advance was the introduction of the metallic rimfire cartridge by Flobert in France in 1845. In effect, the soft copper percussion cap was enlarged and extended so that it could accommodate the priming fulminate in the rim of the cartridge, the propellant powder in the body of the case, and the bullet crimped into the case mouth. Metallic

ABOVE
One of the most powerful cap-and-ball revolvers ever made was the 1847 Walker Colt. Only 1100 originals were produced, but many working replicas like the Italian Uberti are still made in Europe. The muzzle loading cap-and-ball revolver does not use cartridges; black powder propellant is poured in the chambers and a round ball or conical bullet is rammed on top. Ignition is provided by the percussion cap on the nipple at the closed end of the chamber, which blasts a flame into the chamber when hit by the hammer.

cartridges could be used in breech-loading firearms, which were swift to load and reload, and were not significantly affected by weather. The rimfire cartridge proved to be more versatile and effective than the paper-cased needle-fire system designed by Pauly in 1812 or the Lefaucheux pinfire cartridge invented in 1836.

Rimfire cartridges themselves had limitations. The first ones made were low in power, with a calibre of only .22" (5.56mm). The problem lay in the rimfire system itself. The rim of the cartridge had to be weak so that the priming compound could feel the impact of the hammer and ignite the powder charge. Making the cartridge larger was an obvious way to increase the power, but simply using a bigger case and bullet with more powder was not easy. The rim of the case still needed to be thin enough to allow ignition, but strong enough to contain the higher pressures needed to overcome the inertia of a heavy bullet.

One of the most powerful and effective rimfire cartridges made was the .56-56 Spencer. It fired a 350 grain (22.7 g) bullet at 1200 fps (366 mps) with a charge of 45 grains (2.9 g) of black powder. .56-56 Spencer was the first of their big bore rimfire cartridges, which included the calibres .56-52, .56-50 and .56-46. The cartridge was designed for use in the Spencer rifle, which was patented in 1860. Spencer rifles first appeared during the US Civil War in 1862, and were later credited with having given the Union armies a vital firepower advantage prior to their victory at Gettysburg.

Another rimfire cartridge which acquired a well-deserved reputation was .44 Henry. The 15-shot Henry repeater of 1860 was the forerunner of the famous Winchester lever action rifle. The .44 Henry cartridge was not as powerful as the .56-56 Spencer, firing a 200 grain (13 g) bullet at 1125 fps (343 mps). However, it could be used in revolvers, giving frontiersmen the opportunity to have a high-capacity rifle and 6-shot revolver which utilized the same ammunition.

Today rimfire ammunition is only produced in .22 calibre for rifled arms. Its principal uses are for pest control and target shooting.

METALLIC CENTREFIRE CARTRIDGES

In 1866 and 1867 two metallic cartridge designs were created which further revolutionized firearms development. Colonel Hiram S Berdan in the USA designed a strong drawn-brass cartridge case in 1866; its main feature was a separate, sensitive primer pressed into a cavity in the case head. In

LEFT
The Spencer repeating rifle of the American Civil War fired a potent rimfire cartridge and gave the Union armies a considerable firepower advantage at the battle of Gettysburg.

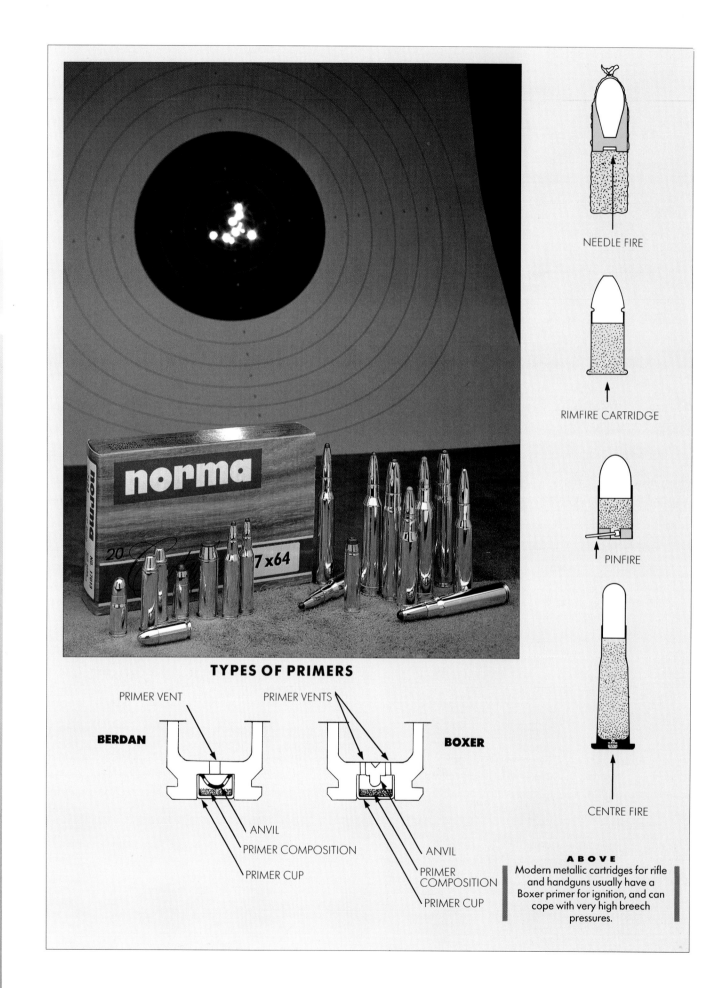

NEEDLE FIRE

RIMFIRE CARTRIDGE

PINFIRE

CENTRE FIRE

TYPES OF PRIMERS

PRIMER VENT

PRIMER VENTS

BERDAN

BOXER

ANVIL

PRIMER COMPOSITION

PRIMER CUP

ANVIL

PRIMER COMPOSITION

PRIMER CUP

ABOVE
Modern metallic cartridges for rifle
and handguns usually have a
Boxer primer for ignition, and can
cope with very high breech
pressures.

England in 1867, Colonel Edward M Boxer made a composite cartridge case with a metal disc head and rolled paper or brass foil case walls. Boxer also used a separate primer, but to improve ignition in his design he used an integral anvil in the primer rather than in the case. The original Boxer design is still used for shotgun cartridges, and it has been modified to use an all-brass, drawn case for rifle and handgun ammunition. It is preferred by shooters who reload their own ammunition. Nevertheless, both designs have a strong case head. They can therefore cope with far higher pressures than their predecessors, and generate higher velocities and muzzle energies.

A B O V E
Black powder (left) gave way to the smokeless propellant cordite (centre left) at the turn of the century. Cordite itself has now been superseded by tubular and flake nitro-cellulose/nitro-glycerine smokeless propellants (centre right and right), and by ball powders (not shown).

SMOKELESS POWDER

The final leap in ammunition technology came with the production of high-pressure 'smokeless' powders made from nitrated wood, cotton or glycerine. With little or no fouling from powder residue, smokeless powders made self-loading firearms possible. Nitrocellulose, guncotton and nitro-glycerine-based propellants also pushed bullet velocities to a different level. Without using big heavy bullets, it was difficult to reach speeds of much more than 1500 fps (450 mps) using black powder in short handgun and rifle barrels. However, with smokeless powders, velocities of 4000 fps (1200 mps) could be attained using small calibre bullets which gave the advantage of lighter weight, lower cost and a flatter trajectory.

CASELESS AMMUNITION

Since 1967 military smallarms development has created weapons which use ammunition with no brass case, where the priming compound and propellant are all consumed during the firing of the round. There is no debris to eject, so ejection ports are not needed. Without a heavy brass case, the ammunition is light in weight, and can be moulded in strips for easy loading. To date, the only working design is that of Heckler & Koch. It has a small, 4.73 mm calibre, and the emphasis is on high cyclic rate and ammunition capacity of the weapon rather than the striking energy of each individual bullet.

One of the current military requirements for rifles is that a 3-shot burst will hit a man at 300 metres. This cannot be achieved with conventional ammunition, but three rounds of caseless ammunition can be fired from the H&K G11 even before recoil forces the rifle to move off aim.

MUZZLE ENERGY

How then do we compare the power of the various types of modern ammunition and the firearms they are to be used in? One of the most popular measurements for comparison is muzzle energy. This is the theoretical energy of the projectile calculated from the square of its velocity, multiplied by the bullet weight, and divided by twice the acceleration of gravity. Muzzle energy is measured in foot-pounds or joules. (One joule being equal to .738 ft lbs.) By using the conversion factor 450240, which incorporates the acceleration due to gravity and the conversion of a bullet weight in grains to weight in pounds, the following formula gives muzzle energy in ft lbs:

$$\text{Muzzle energy} = \frac{\text{Velocity (fps) squared} \times \text{Bullet weight (grains)}}{450240}$$

RELATIVE STOPPING POWER

Muzzle energy is not the only factor in assessing power of a cartridge. The primary objective of a bullet is to kill or incapacitate its target, and the diameter of a bullet also plays a significant part in this. A big bullet travelling at a moderate speed seems to have better 'stopping power' than a small bullet travelling at high speed – even with the same notional muzzle energy. A classic example of this is the comparison between the 9 mm Luger and .45 ACP pistol cartridges. The 9 mm Luger ammunition fires a .353" (9 mm) diameter, 115 grain (7.45 g) jacketed bullet at approximately 1150 fps (350 mps) giving a muzzle energy of 338 ft lbs (458 joules). Some .45 ACP service ammunition (hardball) fires a .451" (11.5 mm) diameter, 230 grain (14.9 g) bullet at 800 fps (243 mps) for 327 ft lbs (443 joules). On the basis of muzzle energy it is claimed that 9 mm Luger is more powerful, yet in

.45 ACP has marginally greater notional muzzle energy than 9mm Luger, but both hollowpoint (left) and ball .45 ammunition have proved far more effective in gunfights than 9mm.

By modifying the bullet design, performance can be improved in the 9mm/.357 calibres, as shown by Lapua's Controlled Expansion Police Projectile (CEPP).

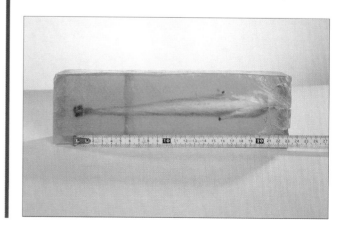

accurately documented fire fights, the .45 ACP hardball has proved time and time again to be far more effective at killing or incapacitating opponents with much fewer shots. One commentator noted that this was because 'big holes let in a lot of air and let out a lot of blood'.

Observations on relative stopping power have led some gunwriters to propose other scales to compare the power of ammunition. One is based on a 'relative stopping power index' and is actually calculated for specific bullet designs. Hollowpoint bullets, for example, expand as they hit flesh, increasing the cross-sectional area of impact. The amount of expansion is affected by velocity, however, and the faster the bullet, the greater the expansion. Hollowpoints work well at rifle velocities of 2000 fps (609 mps) or more, but their performance is variable at handgun velocities of 1000 fps (305 mps) often with incomplete expansion or plugging of the hollow nose as it passes through clothing.

Big game hunters in Africa use the Taylor Knock Out table in calculating the potential effectiveness of a cartridge against dangerous game. The TKO table simply multiplies bullet weight by velocity and bore diameter and divides the result by 7000 to give a manageable figure. (7000 being the number of grains there are in a 1 lb weight). Applying the TKO table to the 9 mm/.45 comparison, rates 9 mm Luger at 6.7 units and the .45 ACP at 11.85, making the ACP nearly 80% more effective.

WHAT IS POWERFUL?

Any discussion on the most powerful firearms in the world must take into account the type of weapon used, and the design and use of the firearm. There are also physical limits to the pressure some breech designs can contain. Of course the ammunition itself is the key to power.

Consider, for example, the .308 Winchester rifle cartridge (also known as 7.62 mm NATO). Until recently this was the standard issue service rifle cartridge for NATO armies. It is also a very effective hunting round, typically firing a 150 grain (9.7 g) bullet at 2860 fps (872 mps) giving an energy of 2725 ft lbs (3690 joules) and a TKO index of 18.9. In normal service or hunting rifles, the cartridge has moderate recoil and adequate but not excessive energy. Although 'powerful' it cannot compare with the .460 Weatherby Magnum dangerous game cartridge, which generates over 8000 ft lbs (10,840 joules) with a .458" (11.6 mm) diameter 500 grain

BELOW
Springfield Armory's M1A gas-operated self-loading rifles in .308 Winchester have low recoil but high striking energy.

LEFT
.308 Winchester is exactly the same calibre as 7.62mm NATO, until recently the issue ammunition for NATO forces. It is being replaced by .223 Remington (5.56mm NATO) for general use but retained for sniping.

BELOW
The .454 Casull fires the most powerful production revolver cartridges made today and is one of the most potent handguns in the world.

(32.4 gram) bullet travelling at 2700 fps (822 mps) with a TKO index of 89.

A handgun made for .308 Winchester with a shorter barrel would lose approximately 500 fps (152 mps) off the velocity. Despite this the muzzle energy would still be around 1850 ft lbs (2507 joules), 150 ft lbs (203 joules) more than the .454 Casull – which is the world's most powerful production revolver cartridge today.

The perceived power is also relevant to both the shooter and the target. For example, if a .44 Special revolver cartridge is fired in a 20 oz (567 gram) revolver there is heavy recoil

and the handgun torques violently in the hand. Put the same ammunition in an 80 oz (2268 gram) rifle chambered for .44 and the recoil would be slight.

Handguns can be viewed as powerful when they reach muzzle energies of more than 350 ft lbs (406 joules), ideally coupled with a barrel bore of .40" (10mm) and above. Rifles cannot be regarded as powerful unless they have muzzle energies of more than 2000 ft lbs (2710 joules) and a barrel bore diameter of .243" (6mm).

DIVERSITY

The improvements in ammunition in the 19th century coupled with better grade steels for gun parts spawned a number of smallarms designs. In the 20th century these have been consolidated into three groups of rifles and three groups of handguns. Each type will be studied in more detail in the subsequent chapters; however it is worth while to compare the designs briefly at this stage to see where most power can be obtained.

REVOLVERS

The age of powerful revolvers began when Colt made the 1847 Walker. One of the most famous revolvers is another Colt product, the 1873 Single Action Army, known as the Peacemaker. The Peacemaker was produced in a range of cartridge calibres, but the most popular was the .45 Colt, which used a black powder charge. A formidable cartridge that is still with us today as a smokeless round, the .45 Colt was the model for the current most powerful production revolver round, the .454 Casull.

SELF-LOADING PISTOLS

Self-loading pistols became feasible with the introduction of smokeless propellants just before the turn of the century. With heavy reciprocating parts they soon became unpleasant to fire as ammunition power increased. The physical size of ammunition was limited by the size of the grip; the most compact designs used a clip magazine to hold ammunition, which was slipped into the butt of the pistol. Western military

BELOW
Dan Wesson's SuperMag revolvers were designed for the sport of metallic silhouette shooting where heavy steel targets have to be knocked down at extended ranges.

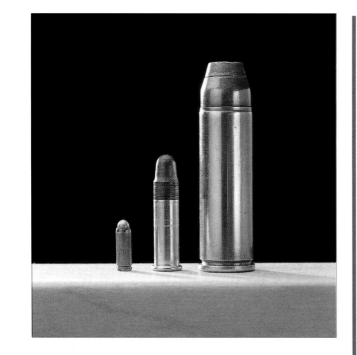

ABOVE
The three handgun cartridges illustrated span the range of pistol power. On the left is 2.7mm Kolibri Auto, a tiny obsolete centrefire pistol round which has less energy than an air pistol (3 ft lbs). In the centre, the .22 LR rimfire cartridge is among the lowest powered of any pistol or rifle ammunition currently made. On the right .454 Casull, derived from .45 Colt, has 30 times the energy of .22 LR and 500 times the energy of 2.7mm Kolibri.

powers soon settled on the 9 mm Luger and .45 ACP calibres as satisfactory for defensive use in self-loading handguns. They also used them for offensive purposes in machine pistols and submachine-guns during the Second World War. Civilians designed more powerful calibres for sporting use in the second half of the 20th century. The most powerful of these is almost certainly the recently launched .50 AE round for use in the Israeli Desert Eagle pistol, which is sold commercially in the West. This firearm will generate approximately 1790 ft lbs (2425 joules) of energy with a 300 grain (19.4 g) bullet.

SINGLE-SHOT HANDGUNS

In the world of single-shot and bolt-action handguns virtually anything can be produced in terms of power and ballistic performance. Many single-shot pistols are simply shortened rifles with a pistol stock. They are popular for handgun hunting and long-range steel plate target shooting. They are also ideal for 'wildcatting', the practice of making new calibres up from existing cartridge cases by increasing or decreasing the bullet diameter, enlarging the case to increase propellant capacity, or shortening the case to give better ballistics from a short barrel.

SINGLE-BARRELLED SPORTING RIFLES

Powerful sporting rifles with a single barrel use a range of different breech types to secure the cartridge during firing.

BELOW
Century Arms revolvers are more powerful still, firing big bore vintage and modern rifle cartridges.

LEFT
The single-shot Thompson Center Contender has interchangeable barrels which are chambered for a wide range of handgun and rifle calibres.

DOUBLE-BARRELLED SPORTING RIFLES

Almost entirely British in origin, the double-barrelled sporting rifle of today has changed little in appearance from those made at the end of the 19th century. Designed for dangerous game shooting in India and Africa, double-barrelled rifles were well-balanced, easy to swing – and utterly reliable. They contained only two cartridges but in the last century the muzzle energy they generated per round with .577 Nitro Express ammunition reached 7000 ft lbs (9485 joules). Double-barrelled rifles are manufactured in even larger calibres today, and their muzzle energies are over 9000 ft lbs (12,200 joules).

HIGH-POWERED MILITARY RIFLES

Military rifles have two applications; for use against enemy personnel, and against enemy equipment. Military conflicts at the turn of the century proved that the most effective rifles against personnel had a calibre of around .30" (7.62 mm) and a muzzle energy of 2500 to 3000 ft lbs (3390–4065 joules). With a rifle in this energy range a soldier could

Many of them are repeating arms using a magazine to feed another round into the chamber as the action is cycled. The most popular guns of this type are bolt action, which derive from the German Mauser actions designed in 1898. The earliest high-powered sporting rifles were the Henry/Winchester lever actions, single-shot Martinis, and various falling block actions. Moderately powered sporting rifles are now made with pump- and gas-operated self-loading actions but the most powerful use bolt actions which, with .460 Weatherby ammunition, are able to reach 8000 ft lbs (10,840 joules).

BELOW
Kimber rifles feature fine workmanship and classic Mauser-type bolt actions.

Italy's largest gunmaker, Beretta,
use Sako actions for their bolt-
action rifles. Their fine double rifles
are wholly produced in Gardone.

The recently produced Holland &
Holland 700 Express can reach a
muzzle energy of over 9000 ft lbs.

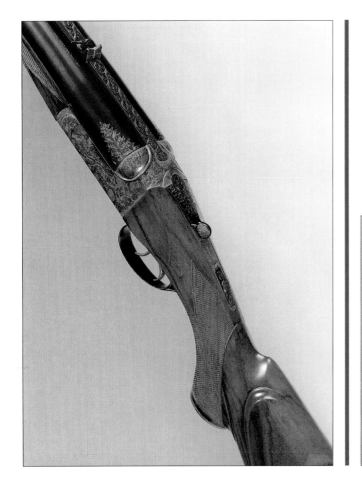

LEFT
The majority of the world's most powerful double rifles, such as those of Westley Richards, are produced in England.

BELOW
Resembling a side-by-side shotgun, double rifles have much heavier barrels and 'Express' sights as shown on the muzzle of this Holland & Holland .500 3" Nitro Express Rifle.

ABOVE
Modern .308 calibre sniping rifles
are accurate at ranges of up to
600 yards, and the ammunition
can penetrate buildings.

penetrate buildings and unprotected vehicles with high velocity ammunition, shooting accurately at ranges of up to 600 yd (550 m). For volley fire against an advancing horde, ranges of up to 2000 yd (1830 m) were used in early conflicts, but bullet-striking energy at that range is minimal.

Two of the most famous and effective rounds of both world wars were Great Britain's .303 British, and the US .30-06 Springfield cartridges; both were used in bolt action rifles and automatic machine-guns. The .30-60 cartridge was also used in the Garand gas-operated rifle, in 1936 – the first self-loading rifle adopted by any army in the world.

The advent of light and medium armour on early tanks used in World War I put new demands on the penetrating power required of smallarms and their ammunition. At first, steel-cored bullets were used in conventional rifles to improve

penetration, but by the beginning of World War II armour had been improved and extremely powerful anti-tank rifles with calibres up to .508" (20 mm) were developed. The best of these could puncture 1.2" (30 mm) of armour with a perpendicular bullet strike. The British .55 Boys round developed in the 1930s had a muzzle energy of 13,722 ft lbs (18,593 joules). The 20 mm Lahti was even more potent with 37,400 ft lbs (50,677 joules) of energy and is still ranked as one of the most powerful weapons that can be fired by one person without a vehicle mount.

By the end of World War II, tank armour had advanced to the stage where only artillery fire or explosive rockets could cause damage to it, and the half-inch military calibres faded from favour. Nevertheless they remain popular with civilian shooters in the USA, particularly rifles chambered for .50 Browning, which can be owned and shot almost without restriction. However, in recent times, there has been a resurgence of interest in .50 Browning for use as a military sniping round – doubtless because of its high energy and very flat bullet trajectory.

ABOVE
Despite its power, the 20mm Lahti anti-tank rifle was ineffective against the tank armour used early on in World War II.

BELOW
50 BMG is now being used for long-range sniping, and for recreational target shooting in the USA. McMillan's M-87R has an efficient muzzle brake to reduce recoil and a 5 round magazine.

2

REVOLVERS

THERE WERE MANY ATTEMPTS TO DESIGN A REPEATING HAND-gun up to the beginning of the 18th century but the idea of a compact, multi-shot personal defence firearm only became feasible with the invention of the percussion cap. Once the method of igniting the propellant was made compact, simple and weatherproof, it was only a short step to the reliable pepperbox revolvers, which appeared around 1820.

PEPPERBOX REVOLVERS

The percussion pepperbox itself was little more than a long cylinder drilled with a number of chambers which rotated around a central pin attached to the single hammer lockwork and butt. The chamber was also the barrel for each bullet, and typically pepperboxes had between four and seven barrels. More sophisticated versions used a cylindrical bushing into which barrels were screwed. This reduced weight, but the principle remained the same – each round had its own un-rifled barrel. At the breech end of each chamber a small hole led to the nipple on to which a percussion cap was placed. These early arms were muzzle-loaded; they did not use metallic-cased ammunition.

A measure of gunpowder would first be poured into each

ABOVE
Smith & Wesson's Model 625 was introduced in 1988 for bowling pin and combat target shooting. Firing the .45 ACP pistol cartridge, it has similar power to revolvers using .45 Colt ammunition.

barrel/chamber and a round ball bullet rammed on top. The first pepperboxes had to have the cylinder rotated by hand to align a fresh chamber to the hammer but by 1837 Ethan Allen in the US patented a trigger-cocking self-indexing model which could be fired repeatedly with one hand.

Nevertheless, there were still a number of disadvantages to the pepperbox; it was expensive to make, heavy to carry, and inaccurate at all but the closest range. The power of the pepperbox design was also limited, being generally of a small calibre for black powder propellant, (typically up to only .40" (10 mm).

COLT'S REVOLVER

The shortcomings of the pepperbox were recognized by Samuel Colt. He patented a 6-shot, hammer-cocked, self-indexing revolver in 1835 in England, and in 1836 in the USA.

Colt had possibly the single greatest influence on the design of the handgun. Many of the principles embodied in his first patents are repeated today in the extremely powerful revolvers now made in North America. In Colt's muzzle-loading revolver a short cylinder was used; just long enough to hold the powder charge, bullet and percussion caps. The cylinder rotated around a central axis (as had the pepperboxes) but Colt added a single, rifled barrel in line with the firing chamber. This increased accuracy, and reduced weight and manufacturing costs. The cylinder was automatically rotated by cocking the hammer. A lever called a pawl, connected to the hammer, pushed the cylinder round until it was locked with a fresh chamber in line with the barrel. In 1836 Colt founded the Patent Arms Manufacturing Company in Paterson, New Jersey, USA, to make .28", .31" and .36" revolvers based on his patents, but by 1842 Colt's business partner was made bankrupt and the company found itself forced into liquidation.

During 1845 and 1846 the war being fought against Mexico in Texas created a fresh demand for Colt revolvers and Captain Samuel Walker was sent to negotiate with Colt for the production of a heavy, open frame .44 calibre black powder percussion revolver. The result was the Army Revolver Model 1847 (Walker), often referred to as the Whitneyville Walker after the town where it was made. Colt no longer had any production capability, so he contracted out the manufacture of the 1847 Army Model to Eli Whitney Jnr. of Whitneyville, New England. Whitney's father had introduced the modern concept of mechanized production of firearms with interchangeable parts to the family business, and he ran a highly efficient factory. The 1847 Walker Colt was indeed a large and powerful revolver, firing a 140 grain (9 g) round lead ball at 1200 fps (366 mps). The 450 ft lbs (610 joules) muzzle energy generated by the Walker is still impressive today, and many working replicas of it are made in Italy. There were only 1100 original Walker Colts produced, but the success of the design enabled Colt to re-establish himself with a new factory in Hartford, Connecticut where he produced similar .44 calibre Dragoon revolvers.

SMITH & WESSON AND METALLIC CARTRIDGES

Manufacture of similar self-indexing revolvers was prevented by Colt's patents in the US until they expired in 1857. By then Horace Smith and Daniel Baird Wesson had begun their second business partnership and set up the Smith & Wesson Revolver Factory in Springfield, Massachusetts. Smith & Wesson had acquired the rights to a vital patent which had been filed in the US by Rollin White in 1855. Part of the patent covered a revolver cylinder which was bored right through, thereby permitting the use of metallic cartridges which were loaded from the back of the cylinder rather than loading the separate ammunition components from the front. Smith & Wesson's new revolvers used small calibre, low-powered .22" rimfire ammunition, but the demand was so great that the company soon had orders which would take several years to fill. Part of the popularity came from the ease of loading and unloading using cartridges. Muzzle loaders can only be unloaded swiftly by firing, although they can be made safe by removing the percussion caps. Smith & Wesson introduced a slightly more powerful .32 calibre metallic revolver in June 1861, shortly after the beginning of the American Civil War. Owning the Rollin White patent gave Smith & Wesson a considerable sales advantage over its competitors who were restricted to producing muzzle-loading revolvers throughout the Civil War and for many years after. The company prospered as a result and after the war came to a close in 1865 turned its attention to large calibre revolvers.

.44 RUSSIAN TO .44 MAGNUM

In 1870, the Model 3 American First Model was released for sale by Smith & Wesson, and it was chambered for the .44/100 (.44 American) centrefire cartridge. The US Army Small Arms Board had examined a Model 3 chambered for the .44 Henry rimfire cartridge, but had recommended that the ammunition be changed to centrefire. At this time the Russian government was purchasing arms in the US and took a great interest in Smith & Wesson's new revolver. The Russians initially contracted to purchase 20,000 revolvers in 1871, with some modifications to the design. One of these was critical to the future development of high-powered ammunition. Indeed the modern .44 Magnum cartridge can

ABOVE
The ancestries of the powerful .44 Magnum Smith & Wesson Model 29 (top) and Ruger Super Redhawk (bottom) can be traced back to the Smith & Wesson .44s of the late 1800s (middle).

trace its history back to the first Russian contract. The specification called for a special stepped cylinder and a cartridge that had the bearing surface of the bullet completely enclosed within the case. Until then, virtually all metallic cartridges used a heeled, externally lubricated bullet with the same diameter as the cartridge case. As a result the chamber they were fired from had easily produced parallel walls, but the

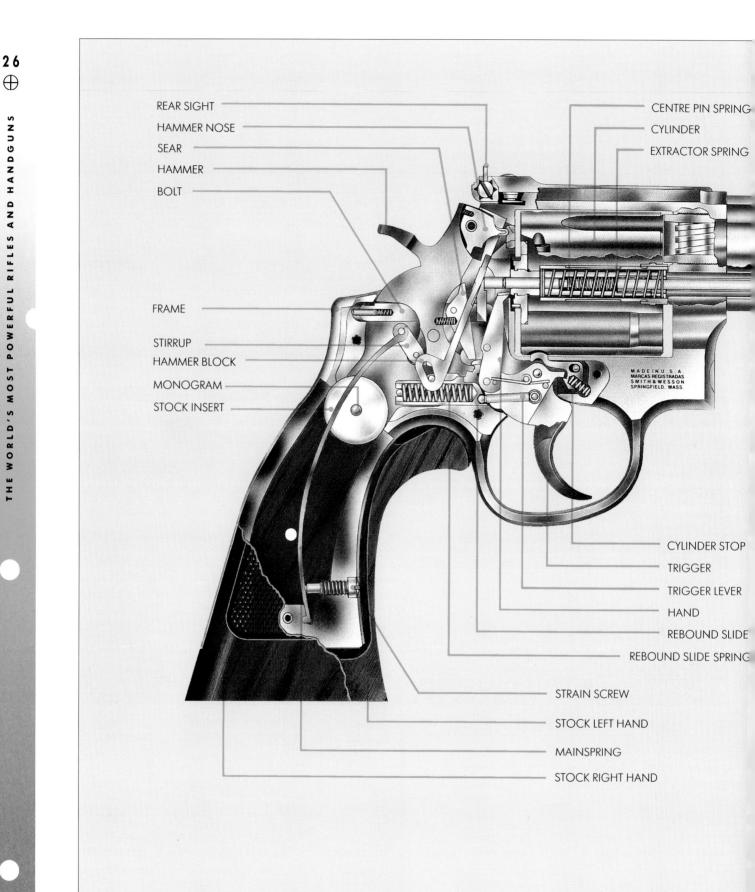

REAR SIGHT

HAMMER NOSE

SEAR

HAMMER

BOLT

FRAME

STIRRUP

HAMMER BLOCK

MONOGRAM

STOCK INSERT

CENTRE PIN SPRING

CYLINDER

EXTRACTOR SPRING

MADE IN U.S.A.
MARCAS REGISTRADAS
SMITH & WESSON
SPRINGFIELD. MASS

CYLINDER STOP

TRIGGER

TRIGGER LEVER

HAND

REBOUND SLIDE

REBOUND SLIDE SPRING

STRAIN SCREW

STOCK LEFT HAND

MAINSPRING

STOCK RIGHT HAND

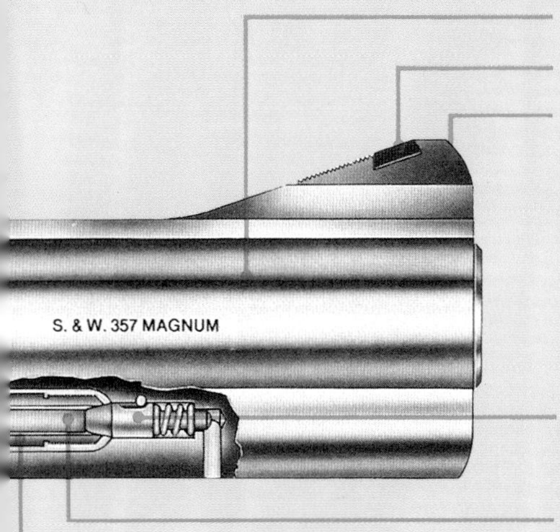

BARREL
COLOURED INSERT
RED RAMP FRONT SIGHT
S. & W. 357 MAGNUM
LOCKING BOLT
CENTRE PIN
EXTRACTOR ROD

LEFT

Smith & Wesson's double-action revolvers are the most popular (and widely copied) in the world.

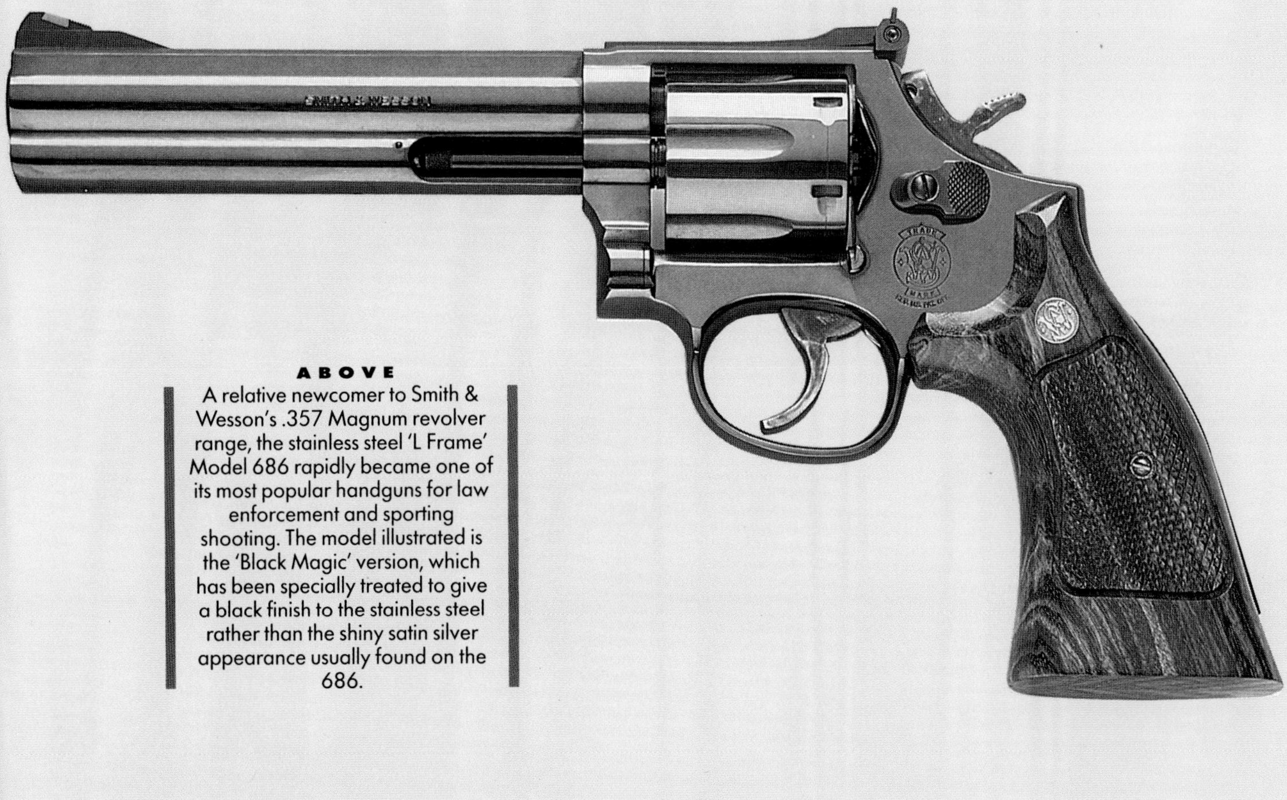

ABOVE

A relative newcomer to Smith & Wesson's .357 Magnum revolver range, the stainless steel 'L Frame' Model 686 rapidly became one of its most popular handguns for law enforcement and sporting shooting. The model illustrated is the 'Black Magic' version, which has been specially treated to give a black finish to the stainless steel rather than the shiny satin silver appearance usually found on the 686.

ABOVE
Modern classics from Smith &
Wesson are their Model 29 (top)
and 629 .44 Magnums.

A B O V E
Ruger's tough single action New
Model Blackhawk in .44 Magnum
is used as the base gun for a
number of even more potent
revolvers.

bullets were prone to damage in storage and the external lubrication attracted dirt. The new cartridge was designated .44 S&W Russian, and generated approximately 325 ft lbs (440 joules) of energy with a 246 grain (15.9 g) bullet. It proved to be extremely accurate and powerful for a black powder cartridge of that period.

TRIGGER-COCKING, SINGLE- AND DOUBLE-ACTION

The Smith & Wesson Model 3 used a single-action trigger like the early Colts. To fire a single-action revolver the hammer has to be thumbed back to full cock before the trigger can be squeezed. Thumbing the hammer back also indexes the cylinder. Another method of firing, trigger-cocking was used on Ethan Allen's pepperbox, and on European 19th-century percussion revolvers, notably those produced by Robert Adams in England. To fire a trigger-cocked revolver the hammer is cocked against a spring and the cylinder rotated by pressure on the trigger. The hammer trips off the sear at the end of the trigger travel, falling on the primer to ignite the cartridge. It takes considerably more force on the trigger to fire a trigger-cocked rather than a single-action revolver: approximately 12 lbs compared to 3–4 lbs. Most popular modern service and target revolvers can be fired by either method, and because they can be shot in two ways they are known as double action. For precision one-handed target shooting the thumb cocked action is used, for action or combat shooting two-handed trigger-cocking is preferred.

.44 SMITH & WESSON SPECIAL

In 1907 Smith & Wesson elongated the .44 Russian case by about .2" in order to accommodate the new bulkier smokeless powders. The original ballistics of the new cartridge, .44 S & W Special, were similar to those of .44 Russian. However,

the energy that could be developed from the cartridge by careful handloading and firing in strong revolvers was far greater. Muzzle energies of 600 ft lbs (813 joules) could be achieved – suitable for hunting.

.44 MAGNUM AND SMITH & WESSON'S MODEL 29

In 1955 Smith & Wesson lengthened the .44 Special case in conjunction with Remington Arms and produced the renowned .44 Remington Magnum cartridge. At the same time S & W launched the Model 29, a large frame, double-action, 6-shot .44 Magnum revolver, generating approximately 970 ft lbs (1314 joules) of energy with a 240 grain (15.5 g) bullet, which achieved the reputation of being the most powerful handgun in the world. Its notoriety was due in part to its use by Clint Eastwood in his 'Dirty Harry' films. The character he played, Inspector Harry Callaghan of the San Francisco Police Dept., was fond of confronting criminals with the considerable bore of his Model 29 and repeating variations on the sentence, 'This is a .44 Magnum 29, the most powerful handgun in the world, it could blow your head clean off.' The publicity this generated substantially improved sales of the Model 29.

When used in a rifle such as Marlin Model 94 lever action carbine, the factory loaded .44 Magnum cartridges can generate over 1500 ft lbs (2032 joules) of energy out of a 24" (610mm) barrel, comparable with many of the early rifle and carbine cartridges that are still in use today.

RANGE OF .44 MAGNUMS

There are now a number of manufacturers producing .44 Magnum revolvers, most of them in the US. Shortly after the introduction of .44 Magnum Sturm Ruger of Southport, Connecticut brought out the single-action Blackhawk models

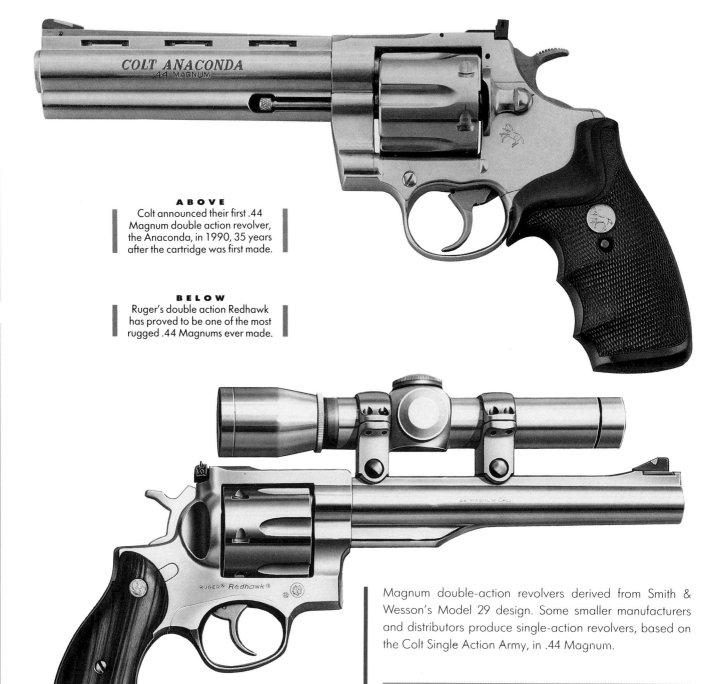

A B O V E
Colt announced their first .44 Magnum double action revolver, the Anaconda, in 1990, 35 years after the cartridge was first made.

B E L O W
Ruger's double action Redhawk has proved to be one of the most rugged .44 Magnums ever made.

and later produced the double-action Redhawk and Super Redhawk .44 Magnum revolvers. In 1990 Colt announced that they would be making a .44 Magnum revolver, 35 years after the introduction of the cartridge. The new handgun known as the Anaconda is made in stainless steel. Dan Wesson Arms of Monson, Massachusetts, USA, produce a version of their large frame double-action revolver in .44 Magnum with interchangeable barrels of different lengths. Astra in Guernica, Spain and Llama of Vitoria produce .44

Magnum double-action revolvers derived from Smith & Wesson's Model 29 design. Some smaller manufacturers and distributors produce single-action revolvers, based on the Colt Single Action Army, in .44 Magnum.

.45 COLT AND THE PEACEMAKER

What the cinema did for the popularity of Smith & Wesson's Model 29 in the latter half of the 20th century, it had been doing for Colt's 1872 'Peacemaker' since the beginning of it. Western films could lead a casual observer to believe that the .45 Peacemaker was the only revolver used in the taming of the American West. Colt had died in 1862, and it had taken the company many years to start producing revolvers to fire metallic cartridges. Incredibly, before Smith & Wesson developed an interest, Samuel Colt had rejected the Rollin White patent when it was offered. Eventually, in 1871, Colt's factory in Hartford began work on their most famous revolver. The 6-shot Single Action Army Revolver was also known as the Model 1873, Frontier or Peacemaker. It remained in con-

ABOVE
Colt began work on the Single
Action Army .45 in 1871 and they
still manufacture it today.

BELOW
Uberti in Italy make replica SAA
revolvers in .45 Colt, and Smith &
Wesson still have the .45 Colt
calibre N-Frame double action
Model 25-5 in their range.

ABOVE
The .454 Casull cartridge was developed from .45 Colt and the 5-shot .454 revolver made by Freedom Arms is both powerful and extremely accurate.

BELOW
Handgun hunters in the USA have taken animals as large as moose with .454 Casull revolvers.

tinuous production until 1940 by which time over 350,000 had been made in almost 30 different calibres. Early production concentrated on calibres that could also be used in lever action rifles, .44-40, .38-40, and .32-20, plus Colt's own powerful new centrefire calibre, .45 Colt. In 1991 Colt put their single-action army revolver back into general release.

The US government adopted the new calibre in 1875 along with the single-action army (SAA) revolver, which remained their issue sidearm until 1892 when they replaced it with the ineffective .38 Long Colt cartridge. The original load for .45 Colt used a 255 grain (16.5 g) lead bullet propelled by 40 grains of FFg black powder to a velocity of 810 fps (247 mps) giving a muzzle energy of 370 ft lbs (501 joules). The cartridge case had considerable internal volume and the later drawn brass cases were quite suitable for the smokeless powders introduced at the turn of the century. Although the factory-produced smokeless rounds only gave a marginal increase in energy – up to just over 400 ft lbs (542 joules) – enthusiastic handloaders were soon generating velocities of 1085 fps (330 mps) with the 255 grain (16.5 g) bullet, giving an energy of 670ft lbs (908 joules).

The versatility of .45 Colt ensures that it is one of the oldest centrefire revolver calibres still in production today, although the number of handguns chambered for it is limited. Although any revolver frame that can take .44 Magnum pressures can be used for .45 Colt, only a handful of manu-

facturers produce suitable cylinders and barrels. Smith & Wesson make the blued-steel Model 25-5 in .45 Colt a double-action large frame revolver similar to the Model 29 .44 Magnum. Ruger make a single-action Bluckhawk in .45 Colt and there are several SAA replicas in the calibre.

DICK CASULL AND THE .454

Two experimenters pushing the .45 Colt cartridge case to its limit were Dick Casull and Jack Fulmer of Salt Lake City, Utah. At the end of the 1950s they modified Colt and Ruger single-action revolvers to take higher pressures and began using duplex and triplex powder loads to produce very high velocities from .45 Colt brass. Like many of the ammunition companies before them they eventually increased the original case length by a small amount to prevent the new high pressure cartridges from being chambered in standard revolvers. The new cartridge was originally called .454 Magnum Revolver, but this was later changed to .454 Casull. High quality 5-shot stainless revolvers based on Colt-style single action frames are made by Freedom Arms of Freedom, Wyoming. They are also known as the .454 Casull after the designer. The promotional video produced by Freedom Arms demonstrated the power and accuracy of the Casull by showing a standing shooter knocking down heavy steel plate targets at 250 yards in one 5-shot string. The .454 Casull is the most powerful *production* revolver cartridge made today, factory loaded ammunition reaching 1725 fps (526 mps) with a 260 grain (16.8 g) bullet. The muzzle energy generated is almost twice that of .44 Magnum at 1730 ft lbs (2344 joules). Despite this however, the Casull is *still* not the most powerful repeating handgun in the world. That distinction could go to one of a number of revolvers or pistols that are chambered for 'wildcat' handmade ammunition, or use vintage big bore rifle cartridges loaded up with modern powders and bullets.

CENTURY REVOLVERS

Without a doubt Century Manufacturing of Greenfield, Indiana, make very powerful revolvers. Originally, the company produced only a heavy 6-shot single-acton revolver chambered for .45-70 Government. The Century Model 100 weighed approximately 6ft lbs (2.7 kg) and had a frame made from high tensile manganese bronze. The .45-70 cartridge has a similar pedigree to that of .45 Colt, originally produced for the US military in 1873. The 45-70 was made for a rifle however – the 'trapdoor' Springfield – and it is only in recent years that it has been increasingly used for hand-

guns. From the Century 100 revolver .45-70 handloads can generate over 2000 ft lbs (2710 joules) of energy depending on the bullet weight.

The company also chambers the Model 100 for three other rifle calibres: .444 Marlin, .30-30 Winchester and .375 Winchester, all of which were originally designed for lever action rifles. Despite the energy of these cartridges, the Model 100 does not recoil excessively.

Century Manufacturing Inc. now make even larger frame 6-shot revolvers to the same design as the Model 100. The Model 500s are chambered for .50-70 Government and 50–110 Winchester, both 19th-century cartridges. The .50-70 Government was the US military rifle cartridge used just prior to .45-70, from 1866 to 1873. The .50-110 Winchester was introduced in 1899 for the Winchester Model 86 lever

RIGHT
Custom pistolsmiths have chambered other revolvers such as the Ruger Super Redhawk for .454 Casull.

action rifle. When loaded with smokeless powder it had comparable energy to some of the British African Game calibres. The Century Model 500 in .50-70 has the trade mark, 'The Mother Load' and from a 10" barrel will push a 535 grain (34.7 g) bullet to 1600 fps (488 mps), developing a muzzle energy of over 3000 ft lbs (4065 joules); higher than that of many high-powered rifles. The manufacturer claims that bullet weights up to 700 grains (45.4 g) can be used, and a muzzle energy of 3500 ft lbs (4742 joules) achieved. The .50-110 version is made to special order, but it is doubtful whether significantly higher energies could be reached with it, because the recoil of the revolver would be too high to allow it to be shot safely.

THE 5-SHOT LINEBAUGHS

One major problem with the Century revolver is its size and weight – being heavier than many sporting shotguns. At the beginning of the 1980s an African big game hunter called Ross Seyfried discussed with John Linebaugh the possibility of producing a high-powered big bore revolver that could be carried on safari and used for big game hunting. Linebaugh had been experimenting along the same lines as Dick Casull with high energy loads based on .45 Colt in modified 6-shot revolvers. Seyfried wanted a handgun for

ABOVE
The big-bore Linebaugh conversions (top and middle) use larger-diameter bullets than the .454 Casull (bottom).

TOP
The .500 Linebaugh revolvers were conceived as hunting handguns, and have proved most effective in thin-skinned game.

ABOVE
Despite a weight of 6 lbs, the recoil
of the .50-70 revolver is
considerable.

BELOW
The accuracy of the Linebaugh
revolvers is more than adequate
for use at short ranges.

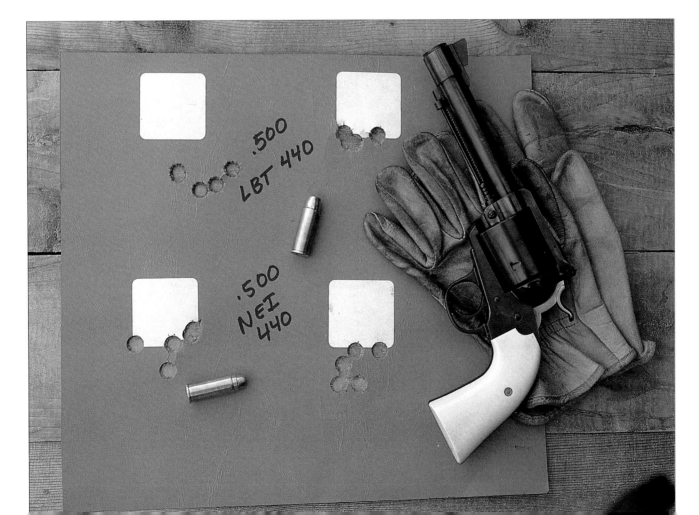

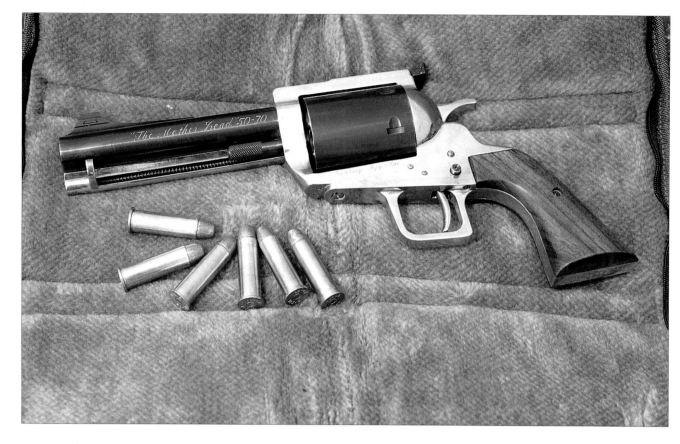

ABOVE
Century Manufacturing offer a choice of barrel lengths and engraving on their revolvers.

TOP OF PAGE
6-shot Century revolvers chambered for .50-70 can produce muzzle energies of over 3000 ft lbs, more than many high powered hunting rifles.

use against lions and Linebaugh had already thought out the design of a .500" (12.2mm) cartridge made from .358 Winchester rifle brass, that would be trimmed to 1.400" (35.6mm) and belled out. To make the handgun Linebaugh started with a Ruger Bisley frame. He fitted a 5-shot stainless steel cylinder that was lined up behind a 6-inch .500" bore barrel. The first handloads used a 385 grain (25 g) bullet which reached 1300 fps (396 mps) – muzzle energy 1445 ft lbs (1958 joules). Accuracy was outstanding: 1½" (38mm) groups were shot from 50 yds (46 m). The load preferred by Seyfried used a 460 grain (29.8 g) bullet travelling at 1200 fps (366 mps) out of the 6-inch barrel with a muzzle energy of 1470 ft lbs (1992 joules), and, importantly for Seyfried, a TKO factor of 41 compared with a .44 Magnum's TKO of 21.

The .500 Linebaugh proved to be excellent for killing thin-skinned game, but it was considered that by increasing the muzzle velocity, and decreasing the cross-sectional area of the bullet, greater penetration of thick hides could be achieved. The result was another 5-shot revolver based on the Ruger Bisley but this time chambered for .475 Linebaugh, a cartridge made by trimming the .45-70 Government case back to 1,400" (35.6mm). With maximum powder loads, the velocity from a 7½" (190.5mm) barrel could reach 1475 fps (434 mps) with a 405 grain (26.2 g) bullet, giving 1830 ft lbs (2480 joules) of energy and a TKO of 39. Accuracy from the .475 Linebaugh revolvers is excellent as well: groups of less than 1 in (25 mm) at 25 yds (23 m) are easily attained, giving an outstanding combination of power and precision.

.357 MAGNUM

The high energies recently achieved by the custom-made revolvers and handmade ammunition tend to overshadow the advances made in high pressure revolver ammunition between the two World Wars. It was shortly after World War I that American law enforcement agencies began dealing with the increasing rise of organized crime in the USA. They requested handguns with greater penetration than their standard issue revolvers and .38 Special ammunition, Smith & Wesson responded by manufacturing a revolver in 1930 based on their heavy N frame used for .44 and .45 revolvers and chambered for .38 Special. Ammunition companies made special high velocity .38 ammunition for use in the tough frames and called it .38-44 S & W Special. The noted writer and ammunition experimenter Philip B Sharpe started developing high velocity loadings for the .38-44 and before long Smith & Wesson became interested in his results. Along with Winchester they produced a new calibre in 1934, .357 Magnum, which in time has become one of the most popular law enforcement and personal defence rounds in existence. The cartridge was ⅛" longer than .38 Special but shared the size same case diameter and rim so that a revolver chambered for .357 Magnum could also chamber and fire lower powered .38 Special ammunition. The first Smith & Wesson .357 Magnum revolver was completed in April 1935 and was presented to J Edgar Hoover, then director of the FBI. The N frame S&W .357 Magnum revolver was later given the model number 27, and it is still in production today.

ABOVE
The two .50-70 cartridges in the centre dwarf the .44 Magnum round on the left. They themselves look up to the .50-110 cartridge on the right.

TOP OF PAGE
Century Arms will also make immense .50-110 revolvers to order.

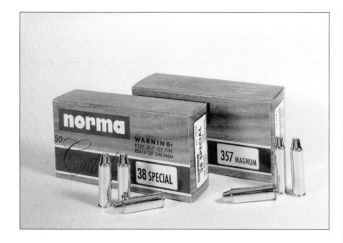

With improvements in the quality of steel it had been possible to produce medium-frame revolvers that can safely fire .357 Magnum ammunition. The original Winchester loads claimed a velocity from 8¾" (222mm) barrel of 1515 fps (472 mps) with a 158 grain (10.2 g) bullet, that gave a muzzle energy of 805 ft lbs (1091 joules), compared with 255 ft lbs (345 joules) for standard 158 grain .38 Special cartridges. Since the introduction of .357 Magnum the pressures and velocities have been reduced in the US and the best energy Winchester now on offer is 583 ft lbs (790 joules) with a 125 grain (8.1 g) bullet travelling at 1450 fps (422 joules). In Europe RWS and Norma still load up to the old standard, with Norma claiming 1490 fps (454 mps) with a 158 grain bullet.

Virtually every centrefire revolver manufacturer in the world produces a handgun chambered for .357 Magnum. In the US Smith & Wesson list seven double-action model types in

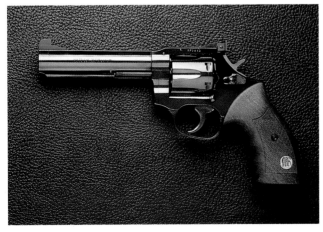

ABOVE
.357 Magnum revolvers are made in Germany by Korth; this is an early 5-shot model.

LEFT
The French arms company, Matra Manurhin, produce a range of .357 Magnum revolvers, some of which have interchangeable cylinders for 9mm Luger.

ABOVE
Apart from the .38 Smith & Wesson
cartridge on the far left, the rounds
illustrated can all be regarded as
powerful in revolvers. The
complete range (from the left) is:
.38 Smith & Wesson .357
Magnum, .357 Maximum,
.41 Magnum, .44 Magnum,
.454 Casull and .50-110 Gov't.

stainless and blued steel, with a total of 20 model/barrel length options. Sturm Ruger list 14 versions of their double-action Model GP100 and six versions of their single-action Blackhawk. Colt sell blue and stainless steel versions of their double-action King Cobra and Python Models. Double-action .357 revolvers are made in Germany by Weirauch and Korth, in Spain by Llama and Astra, in Brazil by Taurus and Rossi, in France by Manurhin, and even in Yugoslavia by Zastava.

.357 MAXIMUM

Heavy .357" calibre bullets at high velocity have a very flat trajectory and have become popular for the sport of metallic silhouette shooting in the US, where steel targets in the shape of animals and bird are shot at extended ranges out to 250 yards. In order to exploit the superior exterior ballistics of .357 bullets, Sturm Ruger and Remington jointly developed the .357 Maximum, which was essentially an elongated .357 Magnum cartridge that ran velocities in vented test barrels of 1825 fps (556 mps) with 158 grain bullets. The revolvers made by Ruger in 1983 and Dan Wesson in 1984 chambered for .357 Maximum suffered from excessive gas cutting of the frame and barrel, and the Ruger was eventually discontinued. The performance of the round was also disappointing, falling 200 fps (61 mps) short of the test barrel velocities when fired in production handguns. The potential of the cartridge has been developed in single-shot pistols however, where there are no cylinder-to-chamber gaps, and therefore no loss of pressure or gas cutting.

.41 MAGNUM

A personal favourite of the author. Despite the success of the .357 and .44 Magnum cartridges, there was a need for an intermediate revolver cartridge for law enforcement, with more stopping power than the .357, but without the blast and high recoil of the .44. The result was the .41 S&W Magnum introduced in 1964 along with the Smith & Wesson Model 57 revolver. Nevertheless, the .41 Magnum proved to be too powerful for many police officers. The handgun was on the same large N frame used for the .44 Magnum model 29, and was rather bulky to carry. As a result .41 Magnum was not a commercial success for law enforcement, but it was enthusiastically received by some sportsmen as a hand-gun hunting cartridge because the lighter bullet gave it better penetration than .44 Magnum with up to 20% less recoil. Muzzle velocity for a 210 grain (13.6 g) bullet in .41 Magnum ranges from 1300–1500 fps (396–457 mps), giving muzzle energies from 790 to 1050 ft lbs (1070–1423 joules). Smith & Wesson still produce two .41 Magnum revolvers, the original Model 57 in blue steel and the 657 in stainless steel. Ruger chamber their Redhawk and Blackhawk revolvers for .41 Magnum and Dan Wesson have also produced models for the calibre.

THE SUPERMAGS

The sport of shooting long-range metallic targets also created another range of high-powered cartridges and revolvers jointly developed by Elgin Gates of the IHMSA (International Handgun Metallic Silhouette Association) and Dan Wesson Arms. The first was the .357 SuperMag, which used a slightly longer cartridge case than .357 Maximum and shot 180 grain

and 200 grain (11.66 & 13 g) bullets at the same speeds as 158 grain bullets out of .357 Magnum. The interchangeable barrels of the Dan Wesson 6-shot revolvers soon had experimenters unscrewing the .357 SuperMag barrels and replacing them with re-threaded .44 Magnum tubes. The cylinder chambers were bored out to take a long version of .44 Magnum ammunition made from .444 Marlin or .30-40 Krag cases that were lathe-turned at the base and trimmed at the mouth to 1.620" (41mm) in length. This high velocity wildcat cartridge was dubbed the .44 UltraMag and could reach velocities of almost 1600 fps (488 mps) with 305 grain (19.8 g) bullets out of a 6-inch (152mm) barrel and a muzzle energy of 1734 ft lbs (2350 joules). By 1989 the various types of the .44 UltraMag were legitimized for use by IHMSA competitors in a version known as the .445 SuperMag, which joined the already established .357 SuperMag and .375 SuperMag. The latter was also a new IHMSA calibre made from shortened .375 Winchester cases trimmed to 1.610" (40.9mm) like the rest of Gates' SuperMags. Dan Wesson made 8" and 10" barrelled double-action revolvers for the new calibres and the IHMSA produced new cartridge cases that did not require trimming and turning. No factory produces complete ammunition since the competitors in IHMSA 'shoots' all hand-load their own rounds, fine-tuning them for accuracy in their own revolvers.

ABOVE
Dan Wesson revolvers like the .445 SuperMag shown have interchangeable barrels and shrouds than can be quickly changed, offering a choice of barrel lengths.

SMALLBORE MAGNUMS

In attempts to develop ultra-high-velocity handgun ammunition, manufacturers tried necking down .357 Magnum brass to smaller calibres in order to use lighter, narrower bullets. These experiments in 1960–61 resulted in two commercial rounds. .22 Remington Jet used a .223" (5.56mm) diameter 40 grain (2.6 g) bullet which reached 2460 fps (750 mps) from an 8½" (216mm) barrelled Smith & Wesson revolver. Despite the high velocity, the light bullet only achieved an energy of 537 ft lbs (728 joules), and the revolvers proved to be unreliable due to the bottlenecked case moving back in the chamber and locking up the cylinder. Winchester made the .256 Winchester cartridge which fired a 60 grain (3.9 g) bullet at 2200 fps (670 mps) to give 645 ft lbs (874 joules) of energy. The bullet could penetrate ¼" (6mm) steel plate, but no handgun manufacturer made a revolver to chamber it. Both cartridges are sometimes found, with limited popularity, in single-shot pistol chamberings.

ABOVE
Despite the short barrel on this
revolver, full power .454 Casull
ammunition generates
considerable recoil, even for an
experienced shooter like gunwriter
John Taffin.

3

SELF-LOADING PISTOLS

.45 ACP has an enviable reputation as a powerful sporting and defence cartridge. Smith & Wesson make stainless steel double-action pistols to fire it. The full size Model 4506 (bottom) has a magazine capacity of eight rounds, the compact Model 4516's magazine holds seven plus one in the chamber.

S ELF-LOADING PISTOLS ONLY BECAME A REALISTIC proposition after the invention of smokeless propellants at the end of the 19th century. Until then, the debris and acid residues left after firing a black powder cartridge soon fouled the intricate moving parts of the (then) experimental semi-automatic handguns. The principal components of smoke-less powders, however, are created by the action of nitric acid on organic chemicals or fibres, which produces nitro-glycerine and forms of nitrocellulose such as guncotton, both of which date from the middle of the 1800s. A Prussian inventor named Shultze made a black powder substitute from nitrated wood in 1865 that achieved limited success. Most of the new propellants could not be used, however, until a simple method of stabilizing them was found by Nobel in the 1870s. Prior to this, the combustion of guncotton and nitroglycerine was too vigorous to be controlled in smallarms. In 1866 the French Army adopted the 8mm Lebel rifle, which used Vielle smokeless powders. Despite their name, smokeless powders do still generate some smoke when fired, it is just considerably less than that generated by black powder, and, importantly, there is no corrosive residue.

BASIC PRINCIPLES

The basic principle of all self-loading firearms is the same. By utilizing either gas produced when fired, or the recoil energy generated by the round, a spent cartridge case is ejected from the breech and a fresh round of ammunition inserted from a magazine. The vast majority of self-loading pistols also re-cock the hammer or striker when cycling. Early military self-loading pistols were single-action only, the hammer needing to be manually cocked before firing. The cocking usually took place as the slide was racked to chamber a round, then a safety catch would be applied.

Modern self-loading pistols of up to 9mm Luger and .45 ACP calibres frequently have a double-action trigger, where a pull on the trigger will cock and fire the gun, and subsequent shots are fired with the hammer cocked by the automatic cycling of the action on firing. There have been a small number of trigger-cocked-only self-loading pistols available, with Smith & Wesson now proposing to offer the facility on its range of self-loaders.

The self-loading action itself occurs in any one of the following ways:

BLOWBACK

Straight blowback is the simplest self-loading system used for pistols. It is used on most low-powered pistols of calibre 9mmK (.380 Auto) and below. The breech holds the cartridge in the chamber by spring pressure. When fired the spring and the inertia of the breech block keep the breech closed until the bullet has travelled most of the way down the normally short barrel, or indeed left it. The breech block, in the form of a slide or bolt, then moves back under recoil, opening the breech. A hooked extractor pulls the spent cartridge out and backwards with the breech block until the rim of the case hits an ejector, which knocks it out through an ejection port. On the forward travel under spring pressure the breech block picks up another round from the magazine and pushes it into the chamber ready for the next shot. Straight blowback is not used for more powerful calibres as either the recoil spring would need to be very strong, or a very large breech-block with a great deal of inertia would be required to keep the action closed during firing. This system is used successfully on machine pistols where weight is not such a problem.

DELAYED BLOWBACK

For higher-powered ammunition the breech of a self-loading pistol needs to be kept positively closed until the bullet has left the barrel and the chamber pressure has dropped. To achieve this a delayed blowback action of some sort must be used. The most common method is the short recoil Browning locked breech design invented by firearms genius John Moses Browning and first patented in 1897. When the slide and breech are fully forward in battery, the barrel is pushed up by a swinging link and lugs on the barrel engage with slots in the slide. On firing, the barrel and breech remain locked and start to recoil backwards together. As the gas pressure drops, the barrel cams down on the swinging link, allowing the slide to travel fully rearwards, extracting the spent case and re-chambering a new one, like a straight blowback pistol. The first design used two links, one at each end of the barrel, but this was later refined into a single link version for a pistol that was made by Colt and adopted by the US Army in 1911. The Model 1911 pistol fired a new

ABOVE
Ruger's new P85 pistol uses a swinging link to effect delayed blowback, just like John Browning did in his original Colt 1911.

powerful cartridge, .45 Automatic Colt Pistol (.45 ACP), and it remained the US military issue sidearm until it was replaced by the 9mm Luger calibre Beretta 92 series pistols in the 1980s. After his death, Browning's design was further refined by Fabrique Nationale in Belgium and in 1935 they produced the GP35 pistol in 9mm Luger which used an angled lug on the underside of the barrel to produce the same locked breech and delayed blowback effect. The other main delayed blowback design still common today is the Walther/Beretta wedge system where a pivoting wedge on the underside of the barrel and slide lock together under the pressure of the gas in the chamber. After recoiling a short distance together the barrel and slide are unlocked by a sliding pin at the rear of the locking wedge. By this time the pressure in the chamber has dropped, and the wedge drops down permitting the slide to move backwards.

Locked-breech, delayed-blowback pistols are made in calibres from 9mm Luger up to .45 Winchester Magnum. Colt have recently acquired the design for a pistol, the Colt 2000, which uses a recoil-operated locked breech similar to that of the gas-operated ArmaLite rifle.

GAS-OPERATED PISTOLS

There have been many unsuccessful attempts to make gas-operated self-loading pistols. They have generally been bulky and complex requiring a powerful cartridge to cycle the action. The breech is usually held shut by a rotating bolt

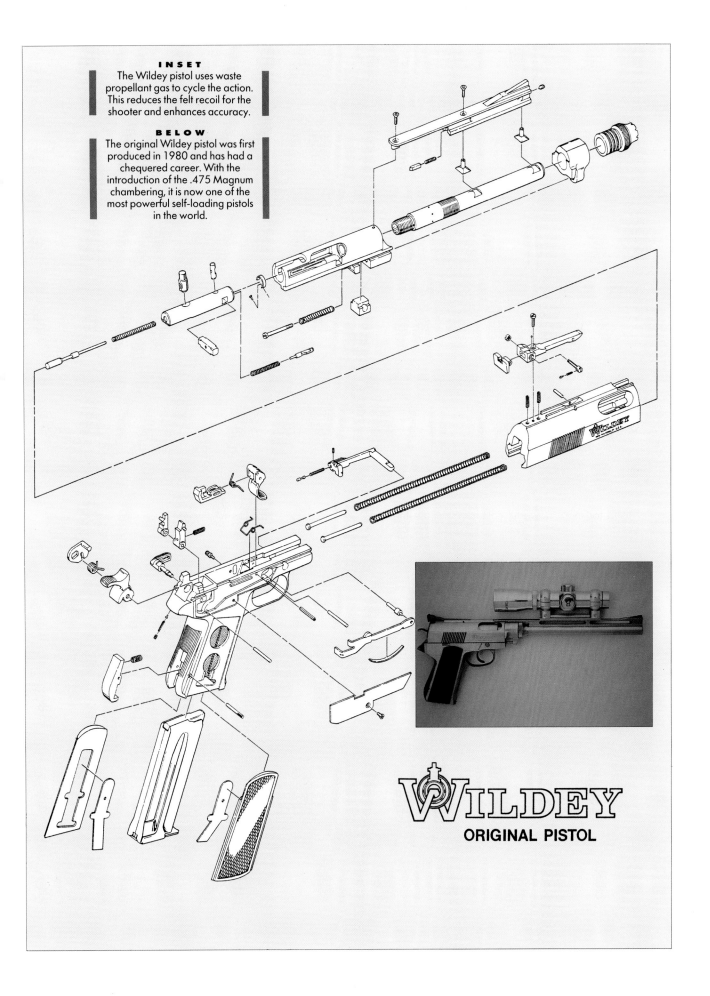

INSET
The Wildey pistol uses waste propellant gas to cycle the action. This reduces the felt recoil for the shooter and enhances accuracy.

BELOW
The original Wildey pistol was first produced in 1980 and has had a chequered career. With the introduction of the .475 Magnum chambering, it is now one of the most powerful self-loading pistols in the world.

WILDEY
ORIGINAL PISTOL

on the slide which locks into lugs in the chamber. Gas is tapped off from the barrel or chamber during firing and pushes against a piston connected to the slide. As in delayed blowback designs, the breech remains closed until the chamber pressure drops and the piston force on the slide causes the bolt to unlock and the slide to cycle the action. The Wildey pistol is still produced using this system as is the Israeli Desert Eagle with which it competes as the world's most powerful production self-loading pistol.

'AUTOMATIC' AND SELF-LOADING REVOLVERS

There have been some notable attempts to produce self-loading, self-cocking or 'automatic' revolvers too, the most famous being the British Webley-Fosbery made between 1901 and 1914. A 6-shot revolver similar in appearance to the self-extracting Webley .455 calibre Mark VI, the Fosbery used the recoil energy of the fired round to index the cylinder and re-cock the hammer. The Fosbery was the most successful of the line of 'automatic' revolvers that had been made at various times throughout the world. One of the earliest was the Spanish Orbea system of 1863, which had a gas port in the barrel and a gas piston, a mechanism frequently found on modern self-loading rifles. In the Orbea revolver a series of levers rotated the cylinder and extracted the fired case. The Paulsen revolver of 1866 also used a gas piston which cocked the hammer and indexed the cylinder.

ADVANTAGES

Apart from the very first models produced, self-loading pistols offered a number of advantages over the revolver. They could hold more ammunition, usually in a detachable clip magazine. The clip magazine meant that they could be re-loaded very quickly by replacing an empty magazine with a charged one. Also, felt recoil from a pistol is generally lower than that of a revolver of the same weight using the same energy ammunition. Some of the recoil is absorbed in the cycling of the action and the pistol can be held closer to the line of the bore reducing the torque during firing. Without a bulky revolving cylinder, pistols are much slimmer than wheel-guns, and without the cylinder to barrel gap, little or none of the propellant combustion gas is wasted.

DISADVANTAGES

There are disadvantages to the pistol as well. A revolver is far quicker to reload from loose rounds and is more reliable with a wide range of ammunition. For a pistol, the ammunition quality has to be consistent otherwise it will fail to extract or to feed. If a cartridge fails to fire for some reason, or there is another malfunction, two hands are usually needed to clear the jam. If a revolver misfires, the action can be thumb-cocked or trigger-cocked with one hand to bring a

fresh cartridge in line with the bore. In the past, revolver actions could generally cope with far higher powered ammunition than a pistol, due to the size of the rounds and the stresses on the reciprocating parts limiting the power of the self-loader. This difference, however, has been whittled down in more recent years.

Pistols require more training to acquire high levels of operational and shooting skill and in military calibres they are generally less accurate than revolvers. Partly for these reasons, the double-action revolver became the preferred handgun for law enforcement and civilian personal defence, and it is only recently that British and American police forces have started to employ the self-loading pistol in preference to the revolver.

MILITARY SPECIALIZATION

Military forces started adopting the self-loading pistol at the turn of the century, having provided the original impetus for its development along with self-loading rifles and automatic machine-guns. Armies have the resources to specify and check the performance of their ammunition, and because 'skill at arms' training is part of their daily schedule, the drawbacks of self-loading pistols diminish. In any event the handgun is usually regarded as a last resort personal defensive weapon for soldiers who prefer artillery and assault rifles as their main firepower. Certain special forces units use handguns offensively for counter-terrorist operations and for hostage release actions at short ranges where machine pistols and rifles are too bulky.

FIRST SELF-LOADING PISTOLS

The first commercial self-loading pistol is believed to be the 8mm Schonberger made in 1892 in Germany. It was derived from a mechanically operated repeating pistol and is believed to use the movement of the cartridge primer during firing to initiate opening of the breech. The first Schwarzlose pistol of 1892 used a low-powered 8mm rimmed cartridge to propel the barrel forwards during cycling. The 1892 pistol was soon replaced by the 1898 model, which had a more conventional rearward sliding breech.

LUGER P'08 PISTOL AND 9mm LUGER CARTRIDGE

In 1893 Hugo Borchardt patented a toggle-jointed pistol based on the Maxim machine-gun whilst working at Ludwig Loewe's factory in Berlin. The frail 'Borchardt' was improved by George Luger, a fellow employee at the company (which later became Deutsche Waffen-und Munitionsfabriken) (DWM), to produce the charismatic Parabellum pistol, more commonly known as the Luger. Originally made in 7.65mm

The rifle makers Mauser also made a charismatic pistol in 1896, known as the Military Pistol Model 1896, which fired the powerful 7.63mm Mauser cartridge. The finely-machined and intricate Model 1896 was nicknamed the 'Broomhandle' after the distinctive grip. Before World War I the Broomhandle became very popular throughout the world and was copied by a number of other manufacturers. In 1917 the Mauser M1896 was made for the German Army in 9mm Luger to supplement the supplies of Luger's P'08. The original calibre for the M1896 used the same dimension bottle-necked cartridge case as Borchardt's pistol (7.65mm Borchardt), but with a larger propellant charge. The bullet weight was light at 85 grains (5.5 g) but the extremely high velocity of 1450 fps (442 mps) gave a muzzle energy of just under 400 ft lbs (542 joules). The Soviet Army adopted the 7.63mm Mauser cartridge in 1930 for use in the self-loading pistol designed by a Fjodor Tokarev and named after him. The designation of the round was changed by the Soviets to 7.62mm Tokarev, even though it had identical performance to Mauser's original.

calibre, the pistol was upgraded in 1902 to fire the new 9mm Luger cartridge and in 1908 was adopted by the German Army as the Model 08 or P'08. The 9mm Luger cartridge eventually became as popular for use in self-loading pistols as the .38 S&W Special did in revolvers. 9mm Luger has become the most common military pistol calibre in the world, being used in handguns and submachine-guns. Despite its popularity, the 9mm Luger, in the author's view, is not a powerful cartridge but merely adequate. The bullet weight is light and travels fast giving high theoretical muzzle energies of just over 300 ft lbs (406 joules), but in documented reports of gunfights the performance of the round is not good and it has now been rejected by the American FBI.

9mm MAUSER EXPORT, MODEL 1908

In an attempt to make more overseas sales of the Model 1896 pistol to Africa, South America and the Oriental East; Mauser introduced a more powerful version of the M1896 in 1908 known as the Export Model. The M1908 used a straight walled 9mm cartridge derived from their 7.63mm round and the new cartridge was named 9mm Mauser Export. This is one of the most powerful production pistol cartridges ever made in Europe and it propelled a 128 grain (8.8 g) bullet to 1361 fps (415 mps) for an energy of 522 ft lbs (707 joules).

THE MARS PISTOL

In 1901 the Birmingham-based pistol designer Hugh W Gabbet-Fairfax submitted one of his Mars pistols to a trial board for consideration as a service pistol. Chambered for a number of unique high energy calibres, the Mars pistol was rejected in 1902 due its large unwieldy size, its tendency to jam, and the change in balance as the slide reciprocated in recoil. At the time it was described as 'a singularly unpleasant and alarming pistol to shoot with'. With no military contract to fulfil, attempts were made to sell the Mars commercially. Without the endorsement of the services however, no one wanted them. Had the Mars survived it would with-

out doubt have been the most powerful self-loading pistol in the world for a considerable time. The 8.5mm Mars cartridge designed by Gabbet-Fairfax fired a 140 grain (9.1 g) bullet at approximately 1750 fps (533 mps) giving an energy of 950 ft lbs (1287 joules); comparable with the modern .44 Magnum revolver. 9mm Mars was equally impressive firing a 158 grain (10.2 g) bullet to 1600 fps (488 mps) for 900 ft lbs (1219 joules), similar in power to the .360 Mars variant. There is no data for 10mm Mars except the bullet weight was 175 grains (11.3 g). The largest four Mars calibres were in .450" (11.4mm) in diameter. The longest and heaviest, .45 Mars Experimental 1, had a case length of 1.303" (33mm) and fired a 260 grain (16.8 g) bullet. Again, there is no other ballistic data on the velocity, but the .450 Mars (long case) ammunition using a shorter case and a 220 grain (14.25 g) bullet is believed to have reached 1200 fps (366 mps).

COLT 1911 AND DERIVATIVES

The heavy 230 grain (14.9 g) bullet of the .45 ACP ammunition produced for the pistol sold by Colt to the US Army as the Model 1911 has proved over many years to be more than powerful enough for personal defence. The theoretical muzzle energy of the cartridge is quite moderate, but the big bore bullet diameter improves the performance. Its 230 grain jacketed round-nosed ammunition, also known as 'hardball', is loaded by the manufacturers to give a velocity of 855 fps (261 mps) for an energy of 405 ft lbs (549 joules). 230 grain armour piercing .45 ACP ammunition can reach 945 fps (288 mps) with an energy of 456 ft lbs (618 joules). Personal defence ammunition like .45 Winchester Silvertip is loaded with 185 grain (12 g) hollowpoints that leave the muzzle at 1000 fps (305 mps) with an energy of 411 ft lbs (557 joules) from a standard 5-inch barrel. Despite the fact that the recoil of the 1911 pistol requires plenty of practice to master, the pistol has been used as a base gun for other high-powered pistols and calibres.

.38 SUPER

The original 7-round Government Model 1911 was slightly modified after World War I and became known as the Model 1911A1. It was additionally chambered for .38 Super in 1929, a high pressure version of the .38 Auto Colt cartridge. The .38 Super fires a 130 grain (8.4 g) bullet at 1280 fps (390 mps) to give an energy of 475 ft lbs (644 joules). Originally .38 Super was not an inherently accurate cartridge since it headspaced on a semi-rim rather than on the case mouth

as in other rimless pistol calibres. During the 1980s .38 Super attracted the interest of IPSC competition shooters who used custom-made rim-headspacing barrels with supported chambers and recoil reducing compensators in their pistols, allowing them to load the cartridge up to the same momentum 'power factor' as .45 ACP. This meant that they could compete in the 'Major Calibre' competition power band, which had a threshold of 175. The IPSC power factor of a cartridge is the product of the muzzle velocity and bullet weight divided by 1000. .45 ACP will reach this factor easily with a 230 grain bullet at 760 fps (232 mps) giving an energy of just under 300 ft lbs (406 joules). To achieve the same power factor in .38 Super with 130 grain bullets requires a velocity of 1346 fps (410 mps). The muzzle energy generated is considerably higher: 523 ft lbs (709 joules). In a pistol fitted with a compensator that uses the waste energy in the propellant gas to push the pistol forwards and down, this high performance round can be light on recoil and very mild to shoot.

LAR GRIZZLY

Another 'stretched' 1911 type handgun is LAR Manufacturing Inc's Grizzly pistol. Made with a variety of barrel and slide lengths the Grizzly is chambered for a number of calibres, the most potent being .45 Winchester Magnum. .45 Win

ABOVE
Springfield Armory produce a number of versions of the 1911A1 pistol, the smallest being their Compact .45.

ABOVE
The Omega pistols from
Springfield Armory have a
universal slide and breech which
can accommodate a number of
different calibres on a basic
1911A1 frame.

MODEL 1911 – A1
CAL 9 mm

ABOVE
For the sport of IPSC Practical Pistol combat target shooting, a factory customized pistol can be bought from Springfield Armory. The model illustrated uses a 9mm slide, but is chambered for the Major power cartridge, .38 Super. The modifications include a compensated, supported chamber barrel to reduce recoil, extended mainspring housing with flared magazine well, hand chequering on the frontstrap, backstrap and trigger guard, oversized magazine release button, extended ambidextrous safety catch, 'beavertail' grip safety, long adjustable trigger, ring-type hammer and adjustable sights.

COONAN .357 MAGNUM AUTOMATIC

In 1980 Dan Coonan of St Paul, Minnesota, USA, began manufacturing a 1911 derived stainless steel pistol chambered for the .357 Magnum revolver cartridge. The Coonan .357 Magnum Automatic uses a longer, deeper frame to accommodate the rimmed cartridge and has a magazine capacity of 7 rounds. The velocity developed by the closed breech of the Coonan is much higher than that of the same round in a revolver.

COONAN™ .357 MAGNUM AUTOMATIC

COONAN™
MAGNUM AUTOMATIC™

ABOVE
The Grizzly pistol is available in a
number of calibres, the most potent
being .45 Winchester Magnum, a
cartridge originally made for the
Wildey pistol.

Mag uses the same 230 grain bullet as .45 ACP but it propels it from a longer case to 1400 fps (427 mps) from the Grizzly to give a muzzle energy of 1001 ft lbs (1356 joules). An even longer .45 rimless cartridge was designed by Winchester in 1984 for the North American Arms Corporation. The .450 Magnum Express had an overall length of 1.753" (44.5mm) and used a 260 grain (16.8 g) bullet reputed to give 1348 ft lbs (1826 joules) energy from a 7.5" (190.5mm) barrel at a velocity of 1525 fps (465 mps).

.451 DETONICS MAGNUM

Almost as powerful as the .450 Magnum Express is .451 Detonics Magnum, made by the Detonics company for their own compact 1911 derived pistol. The Detonics was the same physical size as Colt's pistol, but the very slightly longer ammunition generated far more power. Two loads were produced, one with a 200 grain (13 g) bullet which gave 738 ft lbs (1000 joules) at 1290 fps (393 mps), the other firing a 185 grain (12 g) bullet to 1350 fps (411 mps) for 747 ft lbs (1012 joules). Most of Detonics current production pistols are chambered for .45 ACP but they still list their Scoremaster in the .451 Detonics Magnum calibre. Detonics produce a very compact personal protection pistol for women in .45 ACP that has a powerful punch in a small package.

iAi/AMT AUTOMAGS

A whole series of 1911 derived pistols has been produced by iAi and their trading associates, AMT of Irwindale, California. They initially made the Government and Hardballer pistols, essentially copies of the 1911, firing the same .45 ACP ammunition. This was followed by the 7-inch barrelled .45 ACP, AMT Longslide, which was later chambered in 10mm Auto as well and named the Javelina. iAi acquired the 'Auto-

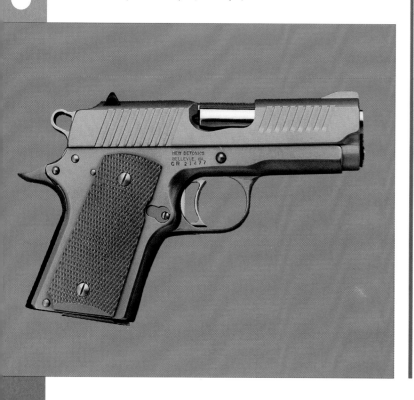

LEFT
Detonics produced a moderately
successful Magnum .45 cartridge
too. The compact and colourful
'ladies' pistols' they now market
are only chambered for .45 ACP,
however, which is powerful
enough.

Mag' name and used that for more pistols in .22 WMR, .30 M1 Carbine and, .45 Win Mag. The Mark 3 in .30 Carbine is the only self-loading pistol in production to use the ammunition that was originally produced for World War II issue .30 carbines issued to US Army troops, although J W Kimball in Detroit, Michigan, USA, developed a 7-shot self-loading pistol for the calibre in 1955. From a 5-inch (127mm) barrel the 110 grain (7.1 g) bullet of .30 Carbine reaches a velocity of 1524 fps (464 mps) and achieves an energy of 567 ft lbs (768 joules).

THE BREN TEN, 10mm AND THE FBI

10mm Automatic was a pistol calibre designed for use in the Bren Ten pistol. Derived from the tough and functional Czechoslovakian 9mm CZ75, the Bren Ten was inspired by combat shooting and self-defence instructor Colonel Jeff Cooper. It was intended to be the perfect combat pistol using a high-powered self-loading cartridge with similar ballistics to the revolver .41 Magnum round. The 11-round pistol was made briefly in the USA in 1983 by the California-based Dornaus & Dixon Enterprises before they ceased trading, leaving a large stockpile of ammunition with Norma in Sweden. By the end of the 1980s other handgun manufacturers awoke to the potential of 10mm Auto, since there had been considerable debate about the effectiveness of 9mm Luger following

a shoot-out between the FBI and two armed bandits in Dade County, Florida. During the gunfight an FBI agent had shot one of the criminals with a 9mm hollowpoint bullet and inflicted a wound to his major organs that informed experts believed would have been fatal even if he had been shot in a fully equipped operating theatre with an emergency medical team standing by. Despite this the criminal still managed to keep on firing his own weapon, killing two FBI agents and wounding six more until he was despatched by a short range shot to the head with a .357 Magnum revolver.

As a result the FBI conducted a series of trials on 10mm Auto ammunition and decided that they would adopt it as their duty round. By this time Colt had made a 10mm version of their 1911A1 pistol named the Delta Elite, and Smith & Wesson tooled up to produce a 10mm Auto derivative of their double action Model 4506 .45 ACP pistol, which they called the 1006. Manufacturers of other 1911 type pistols also made 10mm models and in 1990 Glock launched their Model 20, with a double stacked 15-round magazine. Another European 10mm pistol has been manufactured by Star in Spain, the Star 10, which is available both in a duty pistol specification and as a sporting version with a recoil reducing compensator.

The FBI conducted pistol trials in 1989, which resulted in an initial order for Smith & Wesson of 9,500 handguns based on their Model 1006, but with frame-mounted de-cocking levers and two barrel length options. These were desig-

ABOVE
Colt's first 10mm was the single action Delta Elite, essentially a modified 1911A1 pistol, with a single column magazine.

nated the 1026 with 5½" (140mm) barrel and 1076 with 4¼" (108mm) barrel. During 1990 Frank James, an American gunwriter, carried out an independent endurance test on a stock S&W M 1006. He fired 10,000 rounds of full-power Winchester and PMC factory 10mm Auto ammunition through the gun in just six hours. The barrel reached temperatures of over 400°F and parts of the slide reached more than 230°F. Despite this however, the pistol had only one minor malfunction, and this did not prevent it from completing the test.

During the FBI's proving of 10mm Auto they decided that the original full charge factory ammunition made by Norma was actually too powerful for their application. They eventually chose an ammunition specification which fired a 180 grain (11.7 g) hollowpoint bullet at just under 1000 fps (305 mps) for an energy of 380 ft lbs (515 joules). The FBI specification was unofficially dubbed the '10mm Lite'.

Norma's original offering had a 200 grain (13 g) bullet leaving a 5" (127mm) barrel at 1200 fps (366 mps) with an energy of 635 ft lbs (860 joules), approximately 50% more than the 'Lite' load.

.40 S&W

As a result of the FBI ammunition and pistol tests it became accepted that a .40" (10mm) bullet of just under 200 grains weight travelling at nearly 1000 fps with a muzzle energy of slightly below 400 ft lbs was the optimum 'manstopper'. This is comparable with .45 ACP except that the small bullet

ABOVE
Smith & Wesson made single column 10mm pistols to compete for the FBI contract and they won a large order. The original 1006 (bottom) has a slide mounted safety/decocking lever. One of the models ordered by the FBI, the 1076 (top), uses a frame mounted decocking lever and does not have an additional safety catch.

LEFT
The compact Smith & Wesson 1076, with the lower powered FBI specification 10mm ammunition, has comparable muzzle energy to a full sized .45.

diameter gives better penetration and flatter trajectory. Smith & Wesson jointly developed with Winchester another new cartridge with '10mm Lite' ballistics, called .40 S&W. Essentially a shortened 10mm Auto cartridge, .40 S&W had the advantage that it would fit in magazines made for 9mm Luger calibre pistols. In January 1990 S&W launched the new calibre ammunition along with the Model 4006 and by August 1990 they had secured an order for 7,500 of the pistols from the California Highway Patrol (CHP). During their tests prior to placing the order the CHP subjected all their trial pistols from various manufacturers to a 5,000-round

ABOVE
The ballistics of the FBI load prompted Smith & Wesson to develop another new calibre, .40 Smith & Wesson, and a pistol to fire it, the Model 4006.

BELOW
In competition with Smith & Wesson for American police contracts, Glock also launched a pistol in .40 Smith & Wesson during 1990, the Model 22.

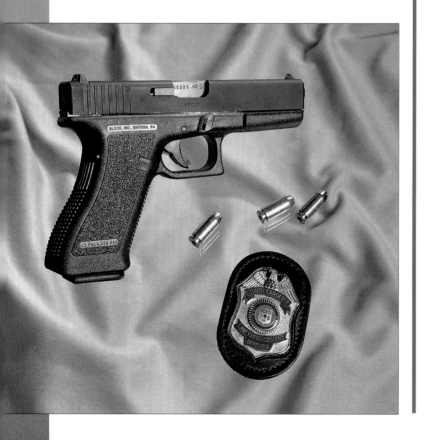

endurance test. The Model 4006 won the endurance test with only two malfunctions.

In the author's view the .40 S&W cartridge is set to become the yardstick law enforcement cartridge for the next decade in the USA, taking over from .357 Magnum. This should come as a great comfort to officers who were being faced with the prospect of exchanging .357 Magnum revolvers for high capacity 9mm Luger self-loading pistols in a wave of re-equipment by US police forces.

.41 AE

Shortly after the demise of Dornaus & Dixon, the Action Arms Company in the US financed the development of .41 calibre pistol cartridge named .41 Action Express (.41 AE) with slightly reduced power compared to 10mm Auto. The cartridge case had a rebated rim the same diameter as 9mm Luger and the nominal bullet diameter was .41" (10.4mm) so that in theory bullets from .41 Magnum revolver cartridges could be used. The rebated 9mm size rim meant that by changing the barrel in a 9mm pistol to .41 AE, the new ammunition could be used at low cost, and without tooling up to produce completely new pistols. The ammunition was made in Israel by Israeli Military Industries, and they chambered their UZI machine pistols for the calibre.

In practice, the ammunition was not initially successful. The .41 AE barrels for standard 9mm pistols had very thin walls, and new magazines were needed with wider lips and a higher feed line to give reliable cycling. Bullet sizes also gave problems, the first ammunition produced in Israel having a bullet diameter of .408" instead of the design specifications: .410" and .411". The frames of some converted 9mm pistols could not cope with the higher energy of .41 AE and eventually the Israelis produced a dual calibre 9mm/.41 AE handgun called the Jericho 941 based on the CZ75 with a longer

frame, heavier slide and much thicker barrel. Tanfoglio in Italy also have purpose-made .41 AE pistols derived from the CZ75, marketed as the 'Ultra' and promoted through the International Practical Shooting Association as a suitable handgun for the combat shooting sport of Practical Pistol. The two factory loadings of .41 AE have either a 170 grain (11 g) bullet travelling at 1225 fps (373 mps) with an energy of 567 ft lbs (768 joules), or a heavier 200 grain (13 g) bullet at a more sedate 1100 fps (335 mps) and an energy of 538 ft lbs (729 mps).

.44 AND .357 AUTOMAG

The original AutoMag pistols were designed by Harry Sanford of Pasadena, California, USA, and were produced in 1970 and 1971 in two calibres: .44 AutoMag (.44 AMP) and .357 AutoMag (.357 AMP). The pistols were constructed

ABOVE
Very few pistols so far have worked well with .41 AE. One that does is the Jericho 941 (bottom) which can be converted to use 9mm Luger in seconds. The Desert Eagle (top) is chambered for the revolver calibres .44 Magnum and .357 Magnum, and an all-new cartridge .50 AE.

from titanium and stainless steel with a 6½" (165mm) barrel and weighed over 65 ounces (1.85 kg) when loaded with a 7-round magazine. Using a 6-lug front-locking rotary bolt, and operating on the short recoil system, they would only work when very clean and using full power ammunition. The first AMP cartridges made were the .44 calibre that were initially produced by cutting down and reaming .308 Winchester (7.62 × 51mm) brass to take the .429" (10.9mm)

LEFT AND ABOVE
Harry Sanford's AutoMag was
short lived, hampered by a lack of
factory ammunition. The first
cartridges were made from cut
down .308 Winchester rifle brass.

diameter bullets used in .44 Magnum revolvers. New .44 brass was produced for a short while in Mexico by Cartuchos Deportivos Mexico, but ammunition was never commercially loaded. The .357 AutoMag ammunition was made by necking down .44 AMP brass to .357 and making a bottle-necked cartridge. Ammunition guru Frank C Barnes lists handloads for .44 AutoMag with a .200 grain (13 g) bullet giving a velocity of 1510 fps (460 mps) and an energy of 1020 ft lbs (1382 joules), and a 240 grain (15.5 g) load at 1275 fps/870 ft lbs (389 mps/1179 joules). The .357 Auto-Mag could use a range of bullets from 110 grains (7.1 g) which reached 1935 fps/918 ft lbs (425 mps/1244 joules), up to 158 grains (10.2 g) which reached 1635 fps/942 ft lbs (498 mps/1276 joules). The AutoMag name has been acquired by iAi in California and is used on part of their range of 1911 type pistols.

WILDEY PISTOL

The Wildey pistol was designed by Wildey Moore and first manufactured by him in Cheshire, Connecticut, USA, in 1980. The business was taken over in 1982 by a New York-based investment group but very few pistols were made until 1987 when Wildey Inc bought back the rights to the design and recommenced production of the Wildey Survivor model in Brookfield, Connecticut. Wildey Moore claims to have made the world's first true gas-operated pistol, and he has chambered it for a mixture of production cartridges and wildcats. By using an adjustable ring around the barrel chamber, the amount of gas used to power the slide can be regulated. This means that the pistol can be fine-tuned to cycle with ammunition of varying power; a great help to shooters who reload their own ammunition.

In 1979 Winchester catalogued the first two calibres for the Wildey: 9mm Winchester Magnum, and .45 Winchester Magnum. The 9mm Win Mag cartridge offered comparable ballistics to the .357 Magnum revolver round, and .45 WM was slightly better than .44 Magnum. Both rounds were essentially lengthened versions of old existing cartridges – 9mm Luger and .45 ACP – and they used the same bullets. The 9mm WM propelled a 115 grain (7.45 g) bullet to 1475 fps (449 mps) from a 5" (127mm) barrel to give a muzzle energy of 556 ft lbs (753 joules), similar to the power of 9mm Mauser Export.

After acquiring the rights back to his original pistol. Wildey Moore set about making the pistol work with some even higher powered ammunition. The first step was the introduction of .475 Wildey Magnum, initially a wildcat cartridge made from cut down and reamed .284 Winchester rifle brass. By 1990 Norma in Sweden had agreed to produce virgin .475 Wildey Magnum brass and Wildey Inc started making ammunition with a 250 grain (16.2 g), .475" (12mm) diameter soft point bullet that would reach 1750 fps (533 mps) from a 10" (264mm) barrel, and an energy of 1700 ft lbs (2303 joules). The African big game hunter's TKO factor for this cartridge is 29.7.

As so often happens with high-powered cartridges, the next stage was to neck down the .475 Wildey Magnum brass to take smaller diameter bullets which would achieve even higher velocities and muzzle energies. A whole family of calibres was designed with a mixture of metric and imperial designations, although they all use imperial calibre bullets. .357 Peterbuilt used 125 grain (8.1 g) and 158 grain (10.2 g) .357 Magnum bullets; 10mm Wildey Magnum used .41 Magnum bullets, and 11mm Wildey Magnum projectiles came from .44 Magnum. The velocities and energies from a 10" (264mm) barrel of all the calibres chambered in the Wildey is as follows:

CALIBRE	BULLET WT		VELOCITY		ENERGY	
	GRAINS	(GRAMS)	FPS	(M/S)	FT LBS	(JOULES)
9mm Winchester Magnum	115	7.45	1475	450	556	753
.357 Peterbuilt	125	8.1	2300	701	1468	1989
.357 Peterbuilt	158	10.2	2060	638	1489	2018
10mm Wildey Magnum	200	13	1842	561	1507	2042
10mm Wildey Magnum	220	14.25	1733	528	1467	1988
11mm Wildey Magnum	200	13	1980	603	1741	2359
11mm Wildey Magnum	240	15.5	1747	532	1626	2203
.45 Winchester Magnum	230	14.9	1540	469	1212	1642
.475 Wildey Magnum	250	16.2	1750	533	1700	2303

Hollywood seems to love featuring the exotic or powerful pistol and in the film 'Death Wish 3', the vigilante character played by the actor Charles Bronson used a Wildey Survivor in .45 Win Mag.

THE DESERT EAGLE AND .50 AE

Israel Military Industries also make a large gas-operated self-loading pistol, the Desert Eagle. This was produced for Magnum Research in the USA and was initially available in two versions which fired the popular revolver cartridges, .357 Magnum and .44 Magnum. The standard barrel on the Desert Eagle could be easily removed and changed for one produced by the factory up to 14" (356mm) long. In .44 Magnum this increased significantly the power that could be generated from the cartridge with the combination of immensely strong rotary locking breech and long barrel with no gas leakage apart from through the gas slide operating mechanism. The author has personally loaded .44 Magnum cartridges with 200 grain (13 g) bullets which reached 1950 fps (594 mps) from the 14" Desert Eagle barrel to give a muzzle energy of 1690 ft lbs (2290 joules); nearly twice that of standard factory ammunition. In 1989 IMI produced the Desert Eagle in .41 Magnum and also chambered some barrels for .357/44 Bain & Davis, a wildcat cartridge.

In 1990 IMI announced an all-new rimless cartridge to be chambered in the Desert Eagle. .50 AE had anticipated ballistics of a 300 grain (19.4 g) bullet travelling at 1632 fps (497 mps) and a muzzle energy of 1792 ft lbs (546 joules). The cartridge and chamber dimensions had to be changed later in 1990 when the American Bureau of Alcohol, Tobacco and Firearms (BATF) declared that the bore of .50 AE was greater than .50" (12.7mm) and that all .50 Desert Eagles would be declared as 'destructive devices' requiring special licensing. The result was a new .50 AE round with a smaller bore and bullet dimension but the same ballistic potential. It will come as no surprise if a necked down version of .50 AE becomes available in something like .44/50 to use heavy .44 Magnum bullets at very high velocities and energies.

ABOVE
The Wildey pistol could be chambered for additional calibres including .475 Wildey Magnum.

BELOW
.475 Wildey Magnum was then necked down to produce .375 Peterbuilt cartridge (2nd left) and the 10mm Wildey Magnum (2nd right) and the cartridge on the left is .357 Magnum; the one on the right .44 Magnum.

4

SINGLE-SHOT HANDGUNS

T HE VERY FIRST HANDGUNS WERE ALL SINGLE-SHOT PIECES, muzzle loaders with black powder and ball for ammunition. The invention of the wheel-lock made it possible to carry one or more reliable handguns for defence, and the later introduction of the flintlock brought down the cost. Reliability was further enhanced by the introduction of the percussion cap at the beginning of the 19th century, signalling the demise of the single shot pistol with the introduction of repeating handguns. It was easier to carry one 6-shot revolver than six, single shot, pistols.

DERINGER

The Deringer pistol made sure that they did not die out entirely. Henry Deringer (the name was later corrupted to 'derringer' and was applied to any small pistol, with one, two or four short fixed barrels), lived and worked in Philadelphia, Pennsylvania, USA, and he made single-shot back action, muzzle loading percussion pistols until his death in 1868. Many of the models had large bores of .41" (10.4mm) and above, and had a short overall length, up to 6" (152mm). The compact size made Deringer's pistols easily concealable and the large calibres made them excellent for short-range personal defence. Despite their popularity and frequent imitators, the single-shot percussion pistols faded out rapidly, like the pepperbox revolvers after the American Civil War, in favour of single-barrel revolvers, and 30 years later, the self-loading pistol.

AMERICAN DERRINGER CORPORATION

The American Derringer Corporation now manufacture the world's widest range of small fixed barrel pistols. Many of them are two barrel models chambered for moderately powered calibres like .38 Spl, 9mm Luger and .32 H&R Magnum but they all have heavy recoil for such a lightweight handgun. There are over 50 calibres available for the Model 1 stainless steel derringer and they include .45 ACP, .357 Magnum, and .45 Colt. American Derringer's Model 4 Alaskan pistol is chambered for two rounds of .45–70 Government, and a special order single-barrelled version can be had in .50–70, evoking the spirit of Henry Deringer. In power to weight terms this is about as powerful as you can get in a handgun, a 16.5 ounce pistol firing a 500 grain bullet. The very short barrel length reduces velocity and energy considerably, but the recoil and muzzle flash are extraordinary. Derringers are renowned less for accuracy than for last resort defence at arm's length. American Derringer have just acquired the rights to the COP pistol, a four-barrelled pistol made in calibres up to .357 Magnum.

SILHOUETTES AND HANDGUN HUNTING

The growing popularity of steel silhouette shooting and handgun hunting in the latter half of the 20th century revived interest in single-shot pistols, but they were quite different from their forebears. The new sports demanded long range accuracy and very high performance ammunition. The pistols needed to be quickly reloadable and chambered for rifle calibres, and they leant themselves to the practice of 'wildcatting' (see next section).

WILDCATS

A wildcat cartridge is one that is not made commercially. Many of the popular sporting cartridges on sale today started life as wildcats, being developed from existing components by professional and amateur enthusiasts. At first, wildcats were mainly improved forms of rifle ammunition. When there appeared to be a need for a better ballistic performance from an action length of barrel bore diameter, the experimenters would take standard cases and reduce or expand the neck size, blow the case out and alter shoulder angles to

ABOVE
The Ultra Light Reb Hunter's pistol has a left-handed rifle action which is easier for a handgunner to use.

increase propellant capacity, or even cut down the overall length of case reforming and reaming the neck. One of the most famous wildcatters was PO Ackley and many of the successful cartridge designs are due to him, the .30–06 Ackley Improved being one of the most popular. If a wildcat becomes very popular, ammunition companies start producing the cartridges for sale and firearms manufacturers chamber their wares for them. .243 Winchester, a popular deer-hunting cartridge started life as a wildcat, as did the rifle cartridges .280 Remington, .308 Norma Magnum, 6mm Remington, and 8mm Remington Magnum. It is worth noting that the new rifle calibres use existing size barrel bores and bullets; it is only the chamber and the case that holds the propellant that are redesigned.

Wildcats for revolvers and self-loading pistols have also been made, the simpler versions usually necking down a large calibre to a smaller one to gain higher muzzle velocity. Some of the recent really high performance cartridges all started life from cut down rifle cases. .375 Super Mag was derived from .375 Winchester, .475 Linebaugh is made from .45–70 brass, .475 Wildey Magnum originally used cut down and reamed .284 Winchester cases; and .44 AutoMag did the same thing with .308 Winchester.

BOLT ACTION

It is no surprise that some of the single-shot pistols made today have essentially Mauser type rifle actions to cope with high pressure ammunition. One of the most popular is Remington's bolt action XP100 chambered for 7mm Bench Rest (7mm BR), a shortened and necked-down version of the rifle calibre .308 Winchester. 7mm BR Ammunition is produced by Remington with a 140 grain (9.1 g) pointed soft point bullet that leaves a 15" (381mm) barrel at 2215 fps (674 mps) with a muzzle energy of 1525 ft lbs (2066 joules). In 1989 Remington introduced 6mm BR ammunition, which used

a lighter 100 grain (6.5 g) bullet which reached 2550 fps (777 mps) and an energy of 1444 ft lbs (1957 joules). 6mm BR has a very flat trajectory, dropping less than six inches (152mm) at 200 yards (183 m). As a comparison, a .44 Magnum handgun firing 240 grain (15.5 g) bullets at 1500 fps (457 mps) would have a 200 yard bullet drop of over 30" 762mm). Remington's XP100 long range pistol is also made in the rifle calibres .223 Remington (5.56mm), .250 Savage, 7mm–08 Remington, and .35 Remington, in left- and right-handed versions. Rifle makers Ultra Light Arms Inc of Granville, West Virginia, USA also make left- and right-handed bolt action pistols based on their rifle action. For a right-handed person it is more convenient to work the bolt of a rifle with the right hand, stabilizing the firearm with the left arm and right shoulder. A long-range handgun has no shoulder stock, however, and it is easier to keep a grip on the butt with the right hand and work a bolt with the left, otherwise the pistol has to be turned on its side to operate the action, or the grip changed. The Ultra Light Hunter's pistol is made in most rifle calibres from .22–250 to .308 Winchester, and it has the advantage of an integral 5-round magazine. Both the XP100 and the Ultra Light have barrels of 14" (356mm) in length and weigh 4 lbs (1.81 kg).

FALLING BLOCK PISTOLS

Falling block actions were popular with rifle makers during the 19th century due to their strength and accuracy. Ruger still produce a falling block rifle and the MOA Corporation of Dayton, Ohio, USA make falling block pistols. The basic design is very simple. A fixed barrel and chamber is closed by a solid bolt of steel that rises up behind the cartridge when a lever in front of the trigger is pulled to the rear. To remove a cartridge the lever is pushed forwards, the steel bolt is lowered and a spring loaded extractor lifts the case a little way out. (This is known as primary extraction.) A fresh cartridge can then be inserted by hand and the bolt closed again. A magazine cannot easily be used with falling block actions, and none are available for current production arms.

Like bolt-action pistols, falling block handguns can be chambered for virtually any pistol or rifle calibre within reason. They both have permanently fixed, screwed in barrels, although the MOA pistol can be supplied with additional factory fitted barrels in other calibres. In order to demonstrate the strength of their pistol, the MOA Corporation have made one chambered for .460 Weatherby Magnum, one of the most powerful bolt-action rifle cartridges made. The handgun was fixed in a machine rest, loaded and fired. There was no damage to the pistol, but the machine rest was ripped from the mountings, and the shooting booth lost some decor due to the muzzle blast. .460 Weatherby is not offered as a standard chambering for the MOA pistol, but there are 20 others to choose from including popular rifle and pistol calibres.

BELOW
Springfield Armory's 1911-A2
SASS conversion turns a 1911A1
self-loading pistol in to a break-top
single shot that can fire rifle
cartridges.

BREAK-TOP PISTOLS

One of the most popular ways to make a single-shot pistol is to use a break-top action, similar to that of a traditional break-top shotgun. The action is kept closed by a cross-bolt and opened with a lever. The barrel tips forward and down, allowing insertion of a cartridge. Lifting the barrel up closes the action which locks shut. To fire, an external hammer must be thumbed back before squeezing the trigger.

One of the main advantages of the break-top pistol is that a single receiver and trigger group can be used with a wide range of barrels. This increases the shooter's calibre options at very low cost. Two US manufacturers, Springfield Armory and Pachmayr, sell conversion kits to change 1911 type self-loading pistols into potent single-shot handguns in a variety of calibres. Springfield's Model 1911–A2 SASS (Springfield Armory Single Shot) has two barrel lengths and eight assorted calibre options, .22 LR, .223 Remington, 7mm Bench Rest, 7mm–08. .308 Winchester, .358 Winchester and .44 Magnum. The most powerful of these is .358 Winchester. From a rifle's 24" (610mm) barrel .358 Win will drive a 200 grain (13 g) bullet to 2530 fps (771 mps). This would probably drop to 1800 fps (549 mps) from the SASS's 14.9" (378mm) barrel if correctly loaded, still giving an impressive 1440 ft lbs (1951 joules) of muzzle energy. The choice of calibres is similar for the Pachmayr Dominator with the exception of .358 Win.

The other manufacturers of break-top pistols are all in the USA. Between them they offer most of the powerful pistol and revolver calibres, and a number of rifle calibres up to .308 Winchester. They include: Competition Arms, Ithaca, RPM, Thompson/Center and Wichita.

THOMPSON/CENTER CONTENDER

The Contender pistol designed in 1967 by Warren Center and manufactured by Thompson/Center Arms is the leading break-top. It was the first modern break-top, and since 1967 has been offered in over 40 chamberings, although the list had reduced to less than half of that by 1990. The calibre options over the six barrel variants are: .22 LR, .22 Win Mag, ¨22 Hornet, .222 Remington, .223 Remington, .270 REN, 7mm TCU, 7–30 Waters, .30–30 Win, .32–20 Win, .357 Magnum, .357 Rem Maximum, .35 Remington, 10mm Auto, .44 Magnum, .445 Super Mag, .45–70 Government and .45 Colt. The .445 Super Mag and .45–70 Government are the most powerful cartridges, but the story of the Contender does not end there.

RIGHT
Single shot pistols can be used for
handgun hunting where a secure
and comfortable holster is
essential.

ABOVE
The Pachmayr Dominator will also convert a 1911 pistol into a powerful single shot handgun.

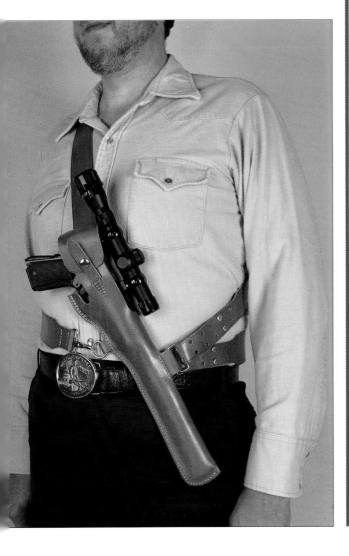

ABOVE
The Thompson/Center Contender was first sold in 1967 and is the biggest selling breaktop pistol in the world, chambered for over 40 standard calibres in its history.

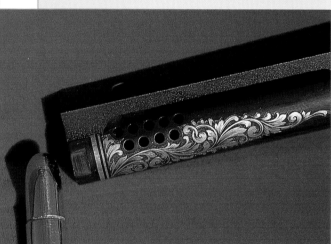

The rugged action of the Contender is used by JD Jones of SSK Industries to build his Handcannon hunting pistols. SSK make new barrels to fit the Contender receiver, and they are chambered for Jones' own wildcat cartridges, which have the suffix JDJ after the calibre. The power of these rounds is remarkable and Jones has used them for hunting all types of game. He is one of the few people to have taken all of the 'big five' African dangerous game with a handgun, a list that includes lion, elephant, and rhinoceros. Three basic cartridges are used for most JDJ wildcats: .225 Winchester (up to 7mm JDJ), .444 Marlin (those larger to .430); and .45–70 (used for .475 JDJ). Both base cases are rimmed to allow easy extraction from the chamber. The most powerful of the JD Jones cartridges, .475 JDJ will reach 1500 fps (457 mps) with a 500 grain (32.4mm) bullet giving an energy of 2500 ft lbs (3388 joules), Jones has made some even 'wilder' wild-cats in his time. One was just .358 Winchester necked up to .375" (9.5mm) and had the name .375 JRS – Jones Rhino Stomper. Another used a shortened and rebated .460 Weatherby case that was belled out to take a .50" (12.7mm) bullet and was made for use in Remington XP action. Jones stopped adding powder when he reached 1800 fps (549 mps) with a 600 grain bullet because he thought the pistol might shake apart with the shock. The muzzle energy generated, 4318 ft lbs (5850 joules), gave considerable recoil in the pistol, which weighed just 5 lbs (2.3 kg), including the telescopic sight. Illustrated is the SCI commemorative pistol, made in 1986 on a Contender action. The detail shows the engraving on the side of the action and the gold inlay at the muzzle, beneath the recoil reducing ports.

THIS PAGE
J D Jones builds his hunting SSK Handcannons on Contender actions. Illustrated is the SCI commemorative pistol made in 1986.

ABOVE
The biggest and toughest game in the world have been shot with handguns, many of them with Contenders and Handcannons modified by Larry Kelly of Mag-Na-Port. The Mag-Na-Port process dramatically reduces felt recoil.

LARRY KELLY AND MAG-NA-PORT

It does not take much imagination to appreciate that handguns firing even moderate rifle cartridges will develop substantial recoil, even out of relatively 'short' 14" and 16" (356mm & 406mm) barrels. In order to reduce the punishment, another handgun hunter, Larry Kelly, designed the Mag-Na-Port system where a series of longitudinal trapezoidal slots are cut in the end of the barrel using Electrical Discharge Machining, or EDM. The slots bleed off some propellant gas just before the bullet leaves the barrel, using it to push the gun forward reducing recoil. There is minimal effect on the bullet velocity and up to 30% reduction in perceived recoil. Most of the Handcannons produced by SSK Industries are Mag-Na-Ported, the two combining to make a powerful and accurate version of the Thompson/Center Contender that is mild to shoot.

ABOVE
The Ordnance Technologies' SSP-91 pistol features a unique rotary breech and is chambered for 17 different rifle and pistol calibres up to .444 Marlin.

SINGLE-BARRELLED SPORTING RIFLES

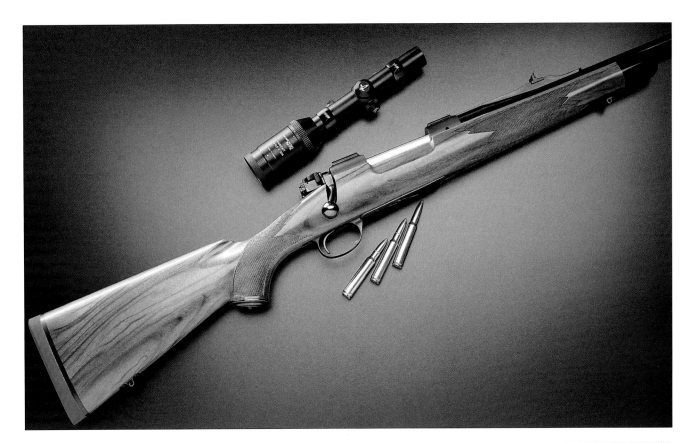

I N THE BEGINNING ALL RIFLES WERE SINGLE-BARRELLED. THE VERY first were small shoulder-fired muzzle-loading cannon, using a smouldering taper to ignite the propellant charge. Ignition systems improved through the matchlock, wheellock, snaphaunce, flintlock and percussion cap until metallic cartridges were achieved in the middle of the 19th century. Along the way, methods of improving firepower were sought and these varied from multiple-barrelled arms to those with multiple charges superimposed in the same barrel with separate sets of flintlocks. The former were heavy and cumbersome, the latter downright dangerous because the risk of igniting all the charges at once was considerable. The invention of effective barrel rifling to spin and stabilize the bullet improved accuracy, and breech-loading metallic cartridges gave the opportunity for high rates of fire. The first breech-loaders were single-shot rifles in which it was necessary to extract or eject the fired cartridge and replace it by hand with a fresh one.

Break-top breech-loaders were generally limited to small low-powered cartridges used for shooting vermin and small game. The British gun trade manufactured stronger actions and then put two barrels side by side for big game hunting in Africa and India. These Double-barrelled rifles are covered in the following chapter.

MARTINI

In order to gain greater strength and to allow the use of more potent calibre, various falling-block actions were produced, the two most famous being the Martini action and the Farquharson falling block. The Martini hinged at the back of the block, swinging down when operated by a lever underneath. A groove in the top of the block assisted the insertion and extraction of the cartridge. Alexander Henry of Edinburgh assisted F Martini of Switzerland in producing a breechloading rifle with the Martini action and Henry rifling. The Martini-Henry was adopted by the British Army in 1871 and it fired the .577/.450 Martini-Henry cartridge which had a 480 grain (31.1 g) bullet in the military loading fired at 1350 fps (412 mps) for a muzzle energy of 1939 ft lbs (2627 joules). The Martini action has been used on a number of European target and military rifles. It is not produced today.

FARQUHARSON

The Farquharson falling-block design is still made by Ruger in the USA for their No 1 rifle. The Farquharson falling block used a solid block of steel that rose vertically in the receiver to close the breech when a lever was operated, making a very tough action indeed. The most powerful cartridge chambered by Ruger in the No 1 is .458 Winchester Magnum. Because of the strength of the design, the No 1 is also used by a number of rifle makers for their own calibres or to revive obsolete ones. The owner of Century Arms in Indiana,

The most effective early lever actions were from Winchester, a company that consolidated the work of American pioneer designers Hunt, Jennings and Henry. Along with the partners Smith and Wesson who later went on to make revolvers in Springfield, Massachusetts, the early designers refined the lever action between 1849 and 1860. Their work culminated in Benjamin Tyler Henry's .44 Rimfire rifle derived from the Volcanic weapons of Smith & Wesson. After the American Civil War, Winchester produced the Model 1866 in .44 Henry Rimfire, an improvement on the first Henry. This was the rifle that became known as 'The gun that won the West'.

Despite their practicality, lever actions were almost totally confined to the US and the opening up of the American West. This was mainly due to the short range of the low-powered ammunition, which could also be used in a revolver. The Winchester Model 1873 was chambered for the moderately powered .32–20; .38-40; and .44–40 calibres.

For military applications, higher powered ammunition was required, and for set piece battles, European armies stuck with big-bore single-shot rifles because of the time honoured method of using them. Ranks of men alternately loaded, aimed and fired on command – often at long range – a system originating from the days of percussion and flintlock muzzle loaders.

As ammunition became more powerful the lever actions had to be strengthened and the locking of the bolt improved to cope with the higher pressures. The 1876 Winchester gave improved performance with the dedicated rifle calibres: .40–60, .45–60, .45–75, and .50–95.

19th-century lever action rifles reached their highest power with ammunition such as .50–110, initially a black powder round introduced in 1899 for the Winchester Model 1886 rifle. The original 110 grain (7.1 g) black powder load pushed a 300 grain (19.4 g) bullet to 1605 fps (489 mps) giving a muzzle energy of 1720 ft lbs (2331 joules). A later smokeless high velocity load drove the same weight bullet to 2225 fps (678 mps) and an energy of 3298 ft lbs (4457 joules), comparable with many of the big game loads used in Africa. It was impractical to use longer and more powerful cartridges in lever actions because of the throw that would be required to empty and reload the chamber. Browning Arms have made limited edition working replicas of the Model 1886.

Winchester's Model 1894 designed by John Browning

has been their most enduring lever action rifle, and is still produced today. The receiver houses an internal falling breech-block that can cope with a wide range of ammunition. The Model 94 is chambered for traditional lever action cartridges such as .30–30 Win and pistol cartridges like .44 Rem Magnum and .45 Colt.

Winchester also make Model 94s in two calibres derived from rimless bolt-action rifle cartridges with the addition of a rim for headspacing. The .307 Winchester round is based on .308 Winchester (known to the military as 7.62mm Nato), and will fire a 150 grain (9.7g) bullet to 2680 fps (817 mps) and an energy of 2393 ft lbs (3243 joules) from a 20" barrel. .357 Winchester is based on the rimless hunting cartridge .358 Winchester and will drive a 200 grain (13 g) bullet to 2400 fps (732 mps) for 2559 ft lbs (3467 joules) of energy from the same length barrel.

In 1896 Winchester began manufacturing the Browning designed Model 1895 that was eventually made in a variety of military calibres like .303; .30–40 Krag; and .30–06. Unlike earlier lever actions, the Model 1896 had a box magazine that permitted the use of ammunition with pointed 'spitzer' bullets. For tubular magazine rifles, ammunition needs a flat-nosed bullet or there is a danger that during recoil the sharp nose of a pointed bullet will hit the primer of a cartridge in front of it with sufficient force to set it off, possibly detonating all the cartridges in the magazine.

ABOVE
Browning made a limited edition
Model 1886 rifle in the 1980s
based on the original Winchester
M1886 in .50-110.

Paul Majors, has re-barrelled a No 1 to .50–70 so that it will use the same ammunition as his Century Model 500 revolvers.

Browning Arms in Morgan, Utah, USA, now make a falling-block rifle based on J Browning's first firearms patent of 1878. The Browning Model 1885 name given to the modern rifle is derived from the name Winchester gave to the original, the Model 1885 High Wall. The most powerful calibre chambered in the rifle is .45-70 Government.

LEVER ACTIONS

There were many attempts to improve the rate of fire of rifles by incorporating a magazine within the body and making a mechanical device to extract the empty cartridge case and reload the chamber. Lever actions were among the first that worked and their method of operation was quite simple. After firing a cartridge, the shooter's hand pushed forward a lever which was an extension of the trigger guard. A mechanical extractor pulled the fired case back out of the chamber and ejected it, re-cocking the hammer at the same time. As the lever was pulled back, a fresh round of ammunition would be lifted from a tubular magazine below the breech and pushed forward into the chamber as the breech closed. With practice, smooth operation of the lever could give a high rate of fire until the magazine ran dry. The rifles were light and narrow, making them easy to carry on horseback.

INSET
The falling block action used in the
Ruger No. 1 rifle is a direct
descendant of the 19th-century
Farquharson.

ABOVE
While the standard calibres for the
Ruger No. 1 stop at .458 Win
Magnum, custom gunmakers have
re-barrelled them up to .50-70.

ABOVE
The Browning 1885 rifle is based
on John Browning's original falling
block patent of 1878.

BROWNING MODEL 81 BLR AND SAVAGE 99

Winchester no longer produce lever action rifles with box magazines, but there are still two other manufacturers who do. Browning make the BLR and Savage, the Model 99. Both have detachable box magazines but the Savage 99 is only chambered for .243 Win. and .308 Win. The Browning Model 81 BLR is chambered for popular rimless sporting calibres up to the .358 Winchester. The considerable strength of the BLR and its ability to cope with high pressure ammunition comes from the seven-lug rotary bolt that locks up tightly in the receiver.

ABOVE
Browning's Model 81 BLR is a modern lever action rifle with a box magazine that is chambered for a range of modern rimless ammunition calibres.

LEFT
Marlin's lever actions with tubular magazines handle cartridges as powerful as their own .444 Marlin. The Model 336 shown is chambered for .30-30.

MARLIN MODEL 444SS

The most powerful of the modern lever action rifles is the Marlin Model 444SS chambered for their own .444 Marlin calibre, which they first produced in 1964. The .444 grew out of the popularity of chambering the .44 Magnum revolver cartridge in lever action rifles for game hunting. The .44 Magnum soon ran out of power for game shooting and had a very rounded trajectory, even in custom handloads. .444 Marlin uses the same diameter bullets but has a longer and thicker case permitting larger powder charges and higher pressures. Factory loaded .444 will give a muzzle velocity of 2400 fps (732 mps) with a 240 grain (15.5 g) bullet that has a muzzle energy of 3069 ft lbs (4159 joules), making it a good short-range 'brush' cartridge.

BOLT ACTIONS

The metallic cartridge case also brought out the potential of the bolt action rifle, which eventually became the world's most popular manually-operated breech-loader. The basic bolt action was first produced in Germany by Johann Niko-laus Dreyse who began work on a new rifle action and system of ignition in 1827. The Dreyse needle-fire rifle was adopted by the Prussian Army in 1840, and while the needle-fire cartridge has been confined to history, the breech-loading system the rifle used is the basis of all modern bolt actions.

Mauser's 1898 type rifle bolt (left) set the standard for others to follow. The .303 No. 4 rifle bolt has lugs at the rear rather than at the front on the Mauser. The Tikka bolt has both for extra strength.

MAUSER 1898

By 1898 Mauser in Germany had refined the bolt action to the point where it has remained in use throughout the 20th century, albeit with a few minor changes. Mauser-type actions are used by virtually all the modern manufacturers of bolt action rifles. The heart of the '98 design is the bolt itself, which has two or more locking lugs on the bolt face and a third one at the back of the bolt. The bolt is essentially a long steel rod with a hole in the middle for the striker and its

spring, a sprung extractor claw to remove the spent case, and an angled operating lever at the rear. The lugs engage in matching lugs in the receiver as the bolt is turned with the operating lever. This mechanically locks together the two parts making a very strong breech that can cope with very high pressures. A slightly different locking arrangement is used in the Austrian Steyr-Mannlicher action which locks at the rear of the bolt with six lugs.

Within the bolt is a spring-loaded firing pin or striker. The striker is cocked as the breech is unlocked by the action of a cam at the rear of the bolt. Pulling the trigger when the action is closed releases the striker, which hits the primer and ignites the cartridge. To reload, the bolt is worked upwards and then backwards, unlocking the breech cocking the striker and extracting the spent cartridge. The empty case is thrown out of the breech at rear of the bolt's travel when it hits an ejector stub. As the bolt is worked forward it picks up a fresh cartridge and pushes it into the chamber ready for the next shot. High rates of fire can be achieved with bolt action rifles, but not quite the rapidity that can be reached with lever actions. The bolt action rifle was the standard service arm of the foot soldier in both World Wars and other lesser conflicts immediately before the turn of the century.

The power that can be generated in a bolt action rifle is very high indeed and original military and commercial Mauser 98 actions are the basis of the high-powered rifles made for use in Africa by Rigby, Holland & Holland and Westley Richards in the UK. These are made for big game hunting and all the manufacturers have at some time designed their own cartridges for use in their branded rifles.

.375 HOLLAND & HOLLAND

Introduced in 1912, Holland & Holland's .375 Belted Rimless Magnum is regarded as one of the most effective medium-bore African cartridges. Holland & Holland still produce bolt action rifles on Magnum Mauser actions chambered for .375 H&H Magnum, as do a host of other manufacturers. The belted case added strength to the web of the cartridge, and many other high performance proprietary and wildcat cartridges have been based on the .375 H&H case. Most ammunition manufacturers produce a .375 H&H load, with a 270 or 300 grain (17.5/19.4 g) bullet. The lighter bullet has slightly more velocity and muzzle energy, 2740 fps (835 mps) and 4500 ft lbs (6098 joules).

Mauser-derived bolt actions are now used almost universally by manufacturers of powerful bolt-action rifles, a) Kimber   b) Beretta c) Browning   d&e) Musgrave f) McMillan.

A ▲

B ▲

D ▼

C ▲

E ▲

▼ F

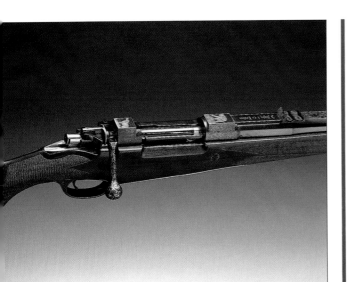

A .30 calibre belted rimless cartridge was introduced by Holland & Holland in 1930 and it became renowned as a fine long range round when the 1000 yard Wimbledon Cup match was won with it in 1935. The velocity and energy of .300 H&H Magnum just exceeds that of .30–06 Springfield.

.416 RIGBY

John Rigby & Co introduced the .416 Rigby cartridge in 1911 for their Mauser Magnum action rifle, and like Holland & Holland they still produce rifles chambered for it today. Since original commercial square bridge Mauser actions are becoming scarce and expensive. Rigby will build a .416 rifle on a choice of actions at the customer's request, including those of Dakota and Ruger from the USA, the Heym from Germany, Dumoulin from Belgium and BRNO from Czecholsovakia. .416 Rigby can be used for all big game and it fires a 410 grain (26.6 g) bullet to 2371 fps (723 mps) for an energy of 5100 ft lbs (6911 joules). Of the American rifle manufacturers, Ruger's Model 77 Magnum is the only one chambered for just .375 H&H and .416 Rigby.

BELOW
Rigby introduced the .416 Rigby cartridge for their rifles in 1911. By the time their 1924 catalogue was produced it had established a reputation as an accurate and powerful big-game round.

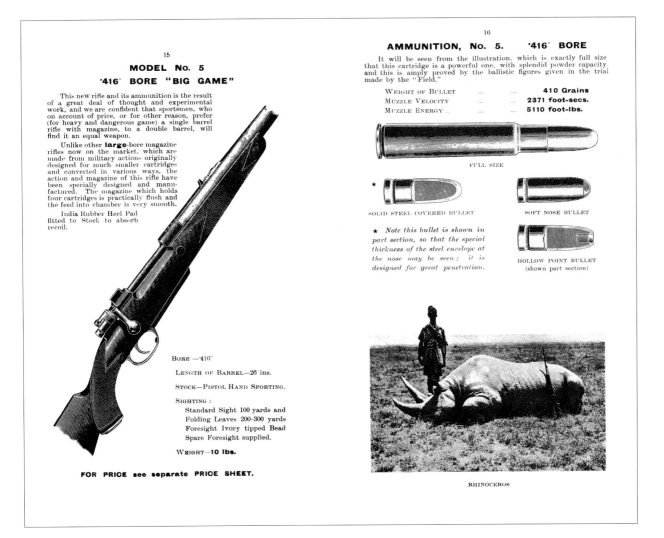

15

MODEL No. 5
'416" BORE "BIG GAME"

This new rifle and its ammunition is the result of a great deal of thought and experimental work, and we are confident that sportsmen, who on account of price, or for other reason, prefer (for heavy and dangerous game) a single barrel rifle with magazine, to a double barrel, will find it an equal weapon.

Unlike other **large**-bore magazine rifles now on the market, which are made from military actions originally designed for much smaller cartridges and converted in various ways, the action and magazine of this rifle have been specially designed and manufactured. The magazine which holds four cartridges is practically flush and the feed into chamber is very smooth.

India Rubber Heel Pad fitted to Stock to absorb recoil.

BORE —'416"

LENGTH OF BARREL—26 ins.

STOCK—PISTOL HAND SPORTING.

SIGHTING :
Standard Sight 100 yards and Folding Leaves 200-300 yards Foresight Ivory tipped Bead Spare Foresight supplied.

WEIGHT—**10 lbs.**

FOR PRICE see separate PRICE SHEET.

16

AMMUNITION, No. 5.   '416" BORE

It will be seen from the illustration. which is exactly full size that this cartridge is a powerful one, with splendid powder capacity. and this is amply proved by the ballistic figures given in the trial made by the "Field."

WEIGHT OF BULLET	...	...	**410 Grains**
MUZZLE VELOCITY	...	...	**2371 foot-secs.**
MUZZLE ENERGY	...	...	**5110 foot-lbs.**

FULL SIZE

★ Note this bullet is shown in part section, so that the special thickness of the steel envelope at the nose may be seen : it is designed for great penetration.

SOLID STEEL COVERED BULLET

SOFT NOSE BULLET

HOLLOW POINT BULLET
(shown part section)

RHINOCEROS

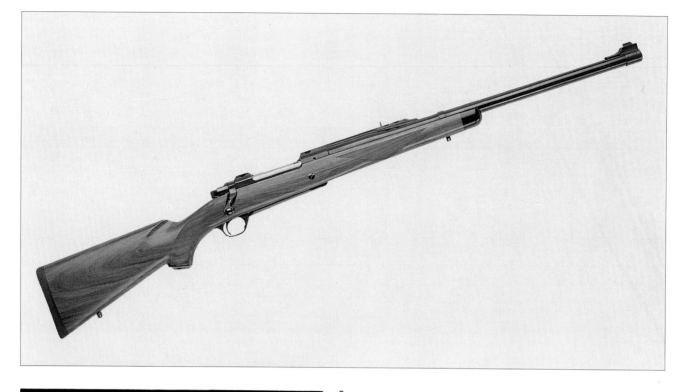

The modern hunter has a large range of ammunition calibres to choose from depending on the quarry, just part of it is shown. From the left: .308 Winchester, 7mm Remington Magnum, .300 Holland & Holland, .425 Westley Richards, .425 Westley Richards Improved, .458 Winchester Magnum, .416 Rigby, .460 Weatherby Magnum.

.425 WESTLEY RICHARDS MAGNUM

The performance of the .416 Rigby is slightly superior to that of .425 Westley Richards, which was first sold in 1909 with a 410 grain (26.6 g) bullet travelling at 2350 fps (716 mps) giving an energy of 5030 ft lbs (6931 joules) – an academic distinction to the animal on the receiving end. The .425 West-

Ruger chamber their Model 77 Magnum rifle for just two calibres, both British, .375 Holland & Holland and .416 Rigby.

ley Richards has a shorter cartridge case than .416 Rigby and does not require the long Magnum action. The first cartridges had a rebated rim to allow the use of a standard Mauser bolt face. There is now an 'Improved' version available with a standard rimless case but it does not have any better ballistics than the original.

OTHER .416 CALIBRES

Many American shooters considered the .416 calibre had become, regrettably, obsolete – despite the fact that ammunition was still loaded for .416 Rigby, and Rigby in London were making the rifles for it. American interest was awakened in 1988 when the .416 Remington Magnum cartridge was produced. It had a belted rimless case that was simply 8mm Rem Mag necked up to hold a 400 grain (25.9 g) bullet, which it powered to 2400 fps (732 mps) for an energy of 5115 ft lbs (6931 joules); little more than that of the Rigby cartridge.

The following year, Weatherby announced their own .416 Weatherby cartridge, which also had a belted rimless case similar to that of Remington's. .416 Weatherby also used a 400 grain bullet but gave a higher velocity of 2700 fps (823 mps) and an energy of 6476 ft lbs (8755 joules) that considerably improved penetration of angled shots on thick-skinned game.

.500 RIMLESS JEFFREY

For many years the .500 Rimless Jeffrey was the most power-ful cartridge available for bolt action magazine rifles. Like .425 Westley Richards it actually had a rebated rim of smaller diameter than the case to fit the bolt face in a Mauser action. The cartridge is, in fact, identical to the German 12.7 × 70 (500) Schuler, both having the same bullet weight: 535 grains (34.7 g), and the same ballistics: a muzzle velocity of 2400 fps (732 mps) and an energy of 6800 ft lbs (9214 joules). The cartridge has been used extensively in Africa in both guises. Jeffrey designed a .400 bore cartridge, known as .404 Rim-less Nitro Express for his magazine rifles. The .404 Jeffrey has been used by RCCM in Canada as the base case for their Imperial Magnum cartridges.

.505 GIBBS RIMLESS MAGNUM

Ballistically slightly inferior to the .500 Jeffrey, .505 Gibbs was introduced just before World War I, and established the unfounded reputation of being a bone breaker when fired. Needless to say, big bore smokeless rifles have a lot of recoil. Mastering that is part of the skill of big game hunting.

EUROPEAN CARTRIDGES

There have been a large number of high powered 'European' (as opposed to British and American cartridges) produced for Mauser action rifles. Some, like 12.7 × 70 Schuler and

7mm Mauser, were interchangeable with Imperial calibres. For example, 7mm Mauser is the same as .275 Rigby. Others are unique: Wilhelm Brenneke designed many cartridges for his own Mauser action rifles in Germany before the First World War; between the wars E A Van Hofe did the same. The most powerful of the Brenneke cartridges is 9.3 × 64, which was available in a number of loadings. The most potent of these has a 293 grain (19.0 g) bullet travelling at 2660 fps (811 mps) which translates as an energy of 4640 ft lbs (6287 joules).

Norma in Sweden introduced their own belted magnum cartridge in 1960 that had slightly better performance than .300 H&H Magnum. The calibre, .308 Norma Magnum uses an Imperial designation in the same way that Lapua do with their sniping/high performance cartridge .338 Lapua Magnum, although the Lapua cartridge does have an addi-tional standard Metric listing, 8.6 × 71mm .308 Norma Magnum has slightly less power than .300 Weatherby Magnum; the conventional rimmed .338 Lapua Magnum is comparable to .340 Weatherby.

WINCHESTER MAGNUMS

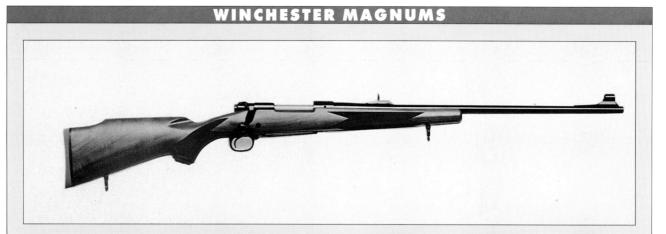

In the USA Winchester produce a considerable range of belted rimless cartridges with the Magnum tag, which has displaced the old term 'Express' for high velocity and high-powered cartridges. In addition to ammunition, Winchester make their Model 70 Sporter and Super Express bolt action rifle for their own and other calibres. The performance data on the belted Winchester Magnums is as follows:

CALIBRE	BULLET WT		MUZZLE VELOCITY		MUZZLE ENERGY	
	GRAINS	(GRAMS)	FPS	(MPS)	FT LBS	(JOULES)
.264 Win Mag	100	6.5	3700	1128	3040	4119
	140	9.1	3200	975	3180	4309
.300 Win Mag	150	9.7	3400	1036	3865	5237
	180	11.7	3070	936	3740	5068
.338 Win Mag	200	13.0	3000	914	4000	5420
	250	16.2	2700	823	4050	5488
	300	19.4	2450	747	4000	5420
.458 Win Mag	500	32.4	2130	649	5040	6829
	510	33.1	2130	649	5140	6965

WEATHERBY

No story on high performance magazine rifles would be complete without the tale of Roy Weatherby and the rifles and ammunition he created. Like many keen hunters, Weatherby began wildcatting, and produced ammunition with a higher performance than that available commercially. In 1937 his experiments with cartridge case capacity and bullet speeds convinced him that the velocity of the projectile was more important than bullet weight or diameter in comparing the relative killing powers of different ammunition. Trajectory was flatter too, and the shock of a very high velocity bullet seemed to bowl thin-skinned animals over quite easily. In 1945, Weatherby began marketing his high velocity cartridges, chambering conventional actions for them. In 1958 Weatherby brought out what he considered to be the best high pressure action for his ammunition. Instead of the conventional two lugs at the bolt face to lock in to the receiver,

Remington Arms Company in Wilmington, Delaware, USA, have a similar range of belted magnum cartridges and chamber their Model 700 rifles for these and other calibres. The Remington Model 700 is used by the US Army as a sniping rifle. The ballistics data of the Remington belted magnums is as follows:

CALIBRE	BULLET WT		MUZZLE VELOCITY		MUZZLE ENERGY	
	GRAINS	(GRAMS)	FPS	(MPS)	FT LBS	(JOULES)
6.5mm Rem Mag	120	7.8	3210	978	2745	3720
7mm Rem Mag	140	9.1	3175	968	3313	4489
	150	9.7	3110	948	3221	4365
	175	11.3	2860	872	3178	4306
8mm Rem Mag	185	12.0	3080	939	3896	5279
	220	14.3	2830	863	3912	5301
.350 Rem Mag	200	13.0	2710	826	3261	4419
.416 Rem Mag	400	26.0	2400	732	5115	6931

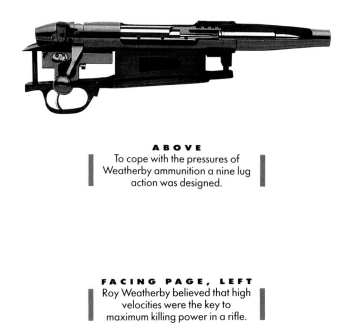

the Mk5 action had nine locking lugs in three groups of three. The end of the bolt is in effect screwed into the receiver as a round is chambered, and the bolt face itself is counterbored to enclose the head of the cartridge case. There are now 10 Weatherby Magnum calibres, all using belted rimless cases. They are all among the most powerful in their calibre class.

The most popular mid-range Weatherby calibres are chambered by a number of manufacturers other than Weatherby themselves. The full list of Weatherby Magnum calibres is: .224, .240, .257, .270, 7mm; .300, .340, .378, .416, and the most powerful of all production magazine rifle calibres at the time of writing, .460 Weatherby Magnum. The big .460 fires a 500 grain (52.4 g) bullet at 2700 fps (823 mps) at the muzzle with an energy of 8092 ft lbs (10,965 joules). At 100 yards the striking energy of .460 WM exceeds the muzzle energy of all but .500 Jeffrey. At 200 yards the energy is greater than the muzzle energy of .416 Rigby and

.425 Westley Richards. At 300 yards the energy is still greater than .338 Win Mag as it leaves the barrel. At 400 yards the striking energy surpasses that of the 7.62mm NATO (.308 Win) military service round at the muzzle.

A-SQUARE WILDCATS

No one cartridge can be called the most powerful for any length of time, because wildcatters are always making new calibres of ammunition. The A-Square wildcats of Arthur B Alphin resulted from the failure of a .458 Winchester cartridge when it was fired at a Cape buffalo in 1974. Alphin set about designing cartridges with more stopping power and based them all on the .460 Weatherby case. Most of the cartridges need the long action and magazine used for Rigby and Weatherby ammunition, except for .460 Short A-Square, which is cut back so that it can be used in the shorter .458 Winchester action.

	BULLETS		VELOCITY in Feet per Second						ENERGY in Foot Pounds						BULLET DROP in Inches From Bore Line			PATH OF BULLET (Above or below Line-of-sight) For riflescopes mounted 1.5" above bore		
	Weight In Grains	Type	Muzzle	100 Yds.	200 Yds.	300 Yds.	400 Yds.	500 Yds.	Muzzle	100 Yds.	200 Yds.	300 Yds.	400 Yds.	500 Yds.	100 Yds.	200 Yds.	300 Yds.	100 Yds.	200 Yds.	300 Yds.
.224 WBY MAG	55	Pt-Ex	3650	3192	2780	2403	2057	1742	1627	1244	943	705	516	370	-1.4	-6.3	-15.6	2.8	3.6	0
.240 WBY MAG	87	Pt-Ex	3500	3202	2924	2663	2416	2183	2366	1980	1651	1370	1127	920	-1.5	-6.4	-15.4	2.6	3.4	0
	100	Pt-Ex	3395	3106	2835	2581	2339	2112	2559	2142	1785	1478	1215	990	-1.6	-6.8	-16.4	2.9	3.6	0
	100	Partition	3395	3069	2766	2483	2216	1966	2559	2091	1698	1368	1091	859	-1.6	-6.9	-16.8	3.0	3.8	0
.257 WBY MAG	87	Pt-Ex	3825	3456	3118	2805	2513	2239	2826	2308	1878	1520	1220	969	-1.3	-5.5	-13.2	2.1	2.9	0
	100	Pt-Ex	3555	3237	2941	2665	2404	2159	2806	2326	1920	1576	1283	1035	-1.5	-6.2	-15.1	2.6	3.3	0
	100	Partition	3555	3292	3044	2810	2589	2377	2806	2406	2058	1754	1488	1254	-1.4	-6.1	-14.5	2.4	3.1	0
	117	Semi Pt-Ex	3300	2882	2502	2152	1830	1547	2829	2158	1626	1203	870	621	-1.7	-7.7	-19.3	3.7	4.6	0
	117	Partition	3300	2998	2717	2452	2202	1967	2829	2335	1917	1561	1260	1005	-1.7	-7.3	-17.6	3.2	3.9	0
	120	Partition	3290	3074	2869	2673	2486	2306	2884	2518	2193	1904	1646	1416	-1.7	-7.0	-16.7	2.9	3.6	0
.270 WBY MAG	100	Pt-Ex	3760	3380	3033	2712	2412	2133	3139	2537	2042	1633	1292	1010	-1.3	-5.7	-13.9	2.3	3.0	0
	130	Pt-Ex	3375	3100	2842	2598	2366	2148	3287	2773	2330	1948	1616	1331	-1.6	-6.9	-16.4	2.9	3.6	0
	130	Partition	3375	3119	2878	2649	2432	2225	3287	2808	2390	2026	1707	1429	-1.6	-6.8	-16.2	2.8	3.5	0
	150	Pt-Ex	3245	3019	2803	2598	2402	2215	3507	3034	2617	2248	1922	1634	-1.7	-7.3	-17.3	3.0	3.8	0
	150	Partition	3245	3036	2837	2647	2465	2290	3507	3070	2681	2334	2023	1746	-1.7	-7.2	-17.1	3.0	3.7	0
7mm WBY MAG	139	Pt-Ex	3400	3138	2892	2659	2437	2226	3567	3039	2580	2181	1832	1529	-1.6	-6.7	-16.0	2.7	3.5	0
	140	Partition	3400	3163	2939	2726	2522	2328	3593	3110	2684	2309	1978	1684	-1.6	-6.6	-15.7	2.7	3.4	0
	150	Pt-Ex	3260	3023	2799	2586	2382	2188	3539	3044	2609	2227	1890	1595	-1.7	-7.2	-17.2	3.0	3.8	0
	154	Pt-Ex	3260	3023	2800	2586	2383	2189	3633	3125	2681	2287	1941	1638	-1.7	-7.3	-17.2	3.0	3.7	0
	160	Partition	3200	3004	2816	2637	2464	2297	3637	3205	2817	2469	2156	1875	-1.8	-7.4	-17.4	3.0	3.7	0
	175	Pt-Ex	3070	2879	2696	2520	2351	2189	3662	3220	2824	2467	2147	1861	-1.9	-8.0	-19.0	3.4	4.1	0
.300 WBY MAG	110	Pt-Ex	3900	3441	3028	2652	2305	1985	3714	2891	2239	1717	1297	962	-1.2	-5.4	-13.5	2.2	3.0	0
	150	Pt-Ex	3600	3297	3015	2751	2502	2266	4316	3621	3028	2520	2084	1709	-1.4	-6.0	-14.5	2.4	3.1	0
	150	Partition	3600	3307	3033	2776	2533	2303	4316	3642	3064	2566	2137	1766	-1.4	-6.0	-14.4	2.4	3.1	0
	165	Boat Tail	3450	3220	3003	2797	2599	2409	4360	3799	3303	2865	2475	2126	-1.5	-6.4	-15.2	2.5	3.2	0
	180	Pt-Ex	3300	3064	2841	2629	2426	2233	4352	3753	3226	2762	2352	1992	-1.7	-7.1	-16.8	2.9	3.6	0
	180	Partition	3300	3077	2865	2663	2470	2285	4352	3784	3280	2834	2438	2086	-1.7	-7.0	-16.6	2.9	3.6	0
	220	Semi Pt-Ex	2905	2498	2126	1787	1490	1250	4122	3047	2207	1560	1085	763	-2.3	-10.2	-25.8	5.3	6.5	0
.340 WBY MAG	200	Pt-Ex	3260	3011	2775	2552	2339	2137	4719	4025	3420	2892	2429	2027	-1.7	-7.3	-17.4	3.1	3.8	0
	210	Partition	3250	2991	2746	2515	2295	2086	4924	4170	3516	2948	2455	2029	-1.7	-7.4	-17.6	3.1	3.9	0
	250	Semi Pt-Ex	3000	2670	2363	2078	1812	1574	4995	3958	3100	2396	1823	1375	-2.1	-9.1	-22.4	1.7	0	-8.0
	250	Partition	3000	2806	2621	2443	2272	2108	4995	4371	3812	3311	2864	2465	-2.0	-8.5	-19.9	1.5 3.6	0 4.3	-6.5 0
.378 WBY MAG	270	Pt-Ex	3180	2976	2781	2594	2415	2243	6062	5308	4635	4034	3495	3015	-1.8	-7.5	-17.8	1.2 3.1	0 3.8	-5.8 0
	300	RN	2925	2576	2252	1952	1680	1439	5698	4419	3379	2538	1881	1379	-2.2	-9.7	-24.0	1.9 4.8	0 5.8	-8.7 0
.416 WBY MAG	400	Swift A-Frame	2600	2365	2141	1930	1733	1552	6003	4965	4071	3309	2668	2140	-2.7	-11.7	-28.3	5.7	6.7	0
	400	RNSP	2700	2391	2101	1834	1592	1379	6476	5077	3921	2986	2249	1688	-2.6	-11.3	-27.9	5.7	6.8	0
	400	Mono Solid®	2700	2398	2115	1852	1613	1402	6476	5108	3971	3047	2310	1746	-2.6	-11.2	-27.7	5.7	6.7	0
.460 WBY MAG	500	RN	2700	2404	2128	1869	1635	1425	8092	6416	5026	3878	2969	2254	-2.6	-11.2	-27.4	2.3 5.6	0 6.6	-9.8 0
	500	FMJ	2700	2425	2166	1923	1700	1497	8092	6526	5210	4105	3209	2488	-2.4	-11.1	-26.9	2.2 5.4	0 6.3	-9.5 0

LEGEND: Pt-Ex=Pointed-expanding. Semi Pt-Ex=Semi pointed-expanding. RN=Round nose. FMJ=Full metal jacket.
NOTE: These tables were calculated by computer using a standard modern scientific technique to predict trajectories from the best available data for each cartridge. The figures shown are expected to be reasonably accurate of ammunition behavior under standard conditions. However, the shooter is cautioned that performance will vary because of variations in rifle, ammunition and atmospheric conditions.
BALLISTIC COEFFICIENTS used for these tables are as published by Hornady and Nosler ballistic data compiled using 26" barrels.

The highest energies generated by the recommended hand-loads in the A-Square range are:

CALIBRE	BULLET WT		MUZZLE VELOCITY		MUZZLE ENERGY	
	GRAINS	(GRAMS)	FPS	(MPS)	FT LBS	(JOULES)
.338 A-Square	300	19.4	2915	888	5600	7588
.460 Short A-Square	500	32.4	2435	742	6580	8916
.495 A-Square	600	38.9	2280	695	6925	9384
.500 A-Square	600	38.9	2452	747	8106	10984

While the .500 A-Square has a lower velocity and muzzle energy than .460 Weatherby, the TKO Factor for it is higher at 105 compared with 89 for the .460. Many believe that this will give the A-Square cartridge the upper hand in the battle for the title of the most powerful sporting magazine rifle cartridge in the world.

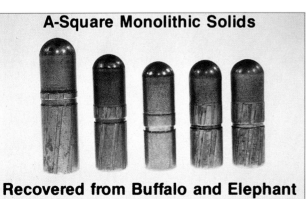

A-Square Monolithic Solids
Recovered from Buffalo and Elephant

ABOVE
A-Square rifles and ammunition were developed by Arthur B Alphin for hunting dangerous game, and their effects were evaluated by him personally. This cow elephant was shot with a Winchester Model 70 rifle converted to .495 A-Square calibre.

LEFT
Different bullet types are used for different quarry. Four of these five monolithic solid bullets were recovered from buffalo and elephant and show no distortion. The central bullet is unfired.

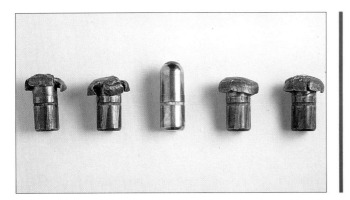

LEFT
The A-Square Dead Tough bullets have a soft point and expand for about one third of the length of the shank, transmitting maximum shock but keeping the bullet components together for maximum penetration.

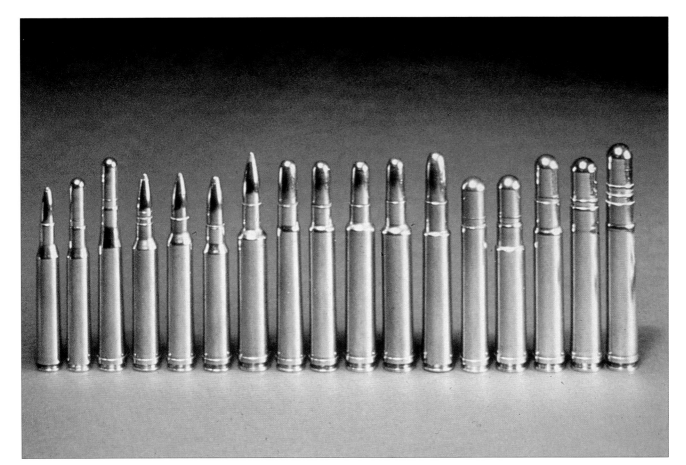

ABOVE
A-Square produce hunting ammunition in their own and proprietary calibres, ranging from .270 Winchester on the left to .500 A-Square on the right.

FACING PAGE, TOP
A-Square Hannibal Model rifle in .338 A-Square Magnum calibre with a Leopold 3×9 telescopic sight.

LEFT
Hunter Bob Haigh with a trophy buffalo, and a 'charger' which came at the sound of shot. The buffalo were killed with one shot each by Haigh using a Hannibal rifle in .500 A-Square.

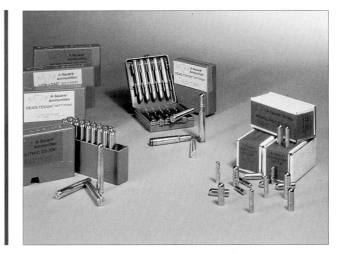

6

DOUBLE-BARRELLED SPORTING RIFLES

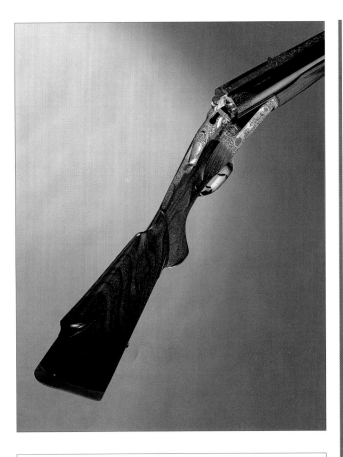

THE WORLD OF THE DOUBLE-BARRELLED RIFLE IS A LONG WAY removed from that of the sporting bolt action rifle or military smallarm. The power that can be achieved by the double rifle is immense, and that is why it is used in Africa and India for the pursuit of dangerous game. A standing marksman will shoot from distances of 100 yards (91 m) right down to a few feet when hunting such animals as elephants, rhinoceros, lion and buffalo. The hunter, equipped with a double rifle, has an unrivalled combination of raw energy and insurance in the event of a cartridge misfiring or simply missing a fast-moving target; with a double rifle, a second shot is available immediately with no need to work a bolt.

The origins of the big doubles lie in the fine English sporting shotguns of the 19th century. Indeed the companies that

LEFT
Westley Richards .458 Winchester Magnum boxlock with doll's head triple-bite lock, deep engraving and coin finish.

BELOW, LEFT AND RIGHT
Rigby's catalogue of 1901 extolled the virtues of their double rifles with .450 calibre ammunition.

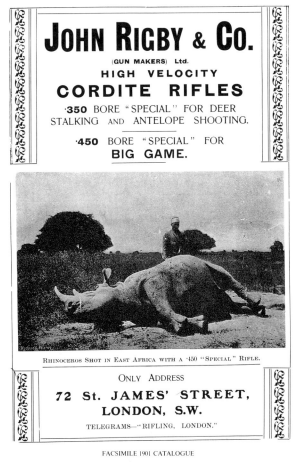

JOHN RIGBY & CO.

(GUN MAKERS) Ltd.

HIGH VELOCITY
CORDITE RIFLES

·350 BORE "SPECIAL" FOR DEER STALKING AND ANTELOPE SHOOTING.

·450 BORE "SPECIAL" FOR **BIG GAME.**

RHINOCEROS SHOT IN EAST AFRICA WITH A ·450 "SPECIAL" RIFLE.

ONLY ADDRESS

72 St. JAMES' STREET, LONDON, S.W.

TELEGRAMS—"RIFLING, LONDON."

FACSIMILE 1901 CATALOGUE

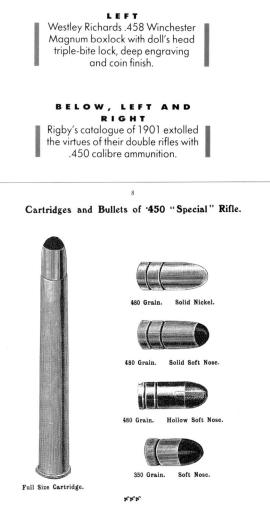

8

Cartridges and Bullets of ·450 "Special" Rifle.

480 Grain.   Solid Nickel.

480 Grain.   Solid Soft Nose.

480 Grain.   Hollow Soft Nose.

350 Grain.   Soft Nose.

Full Size Cartridge.

These "Special" Cartridges are most carefully loaded with the best (selected) cordite, the results obtained are most regular, and the keeping qualities in any climate very good.

Cartridges loaded with 480 grain bullets give a muzzle velocity of 2050 f.s., and striking energy 4512 ft. lbs. And with the 350 grain bullets muzzle velocity 2200 f.s. The sighting being the same for both within sporting ranges.

PRICE OF CARTRIDGES, per 100, 30/-

craft the latter today also manufacture first class double-barrelled shotguns.

The demand for double rifles dropped off between the wars as the British Empire was broken up and reduced in size, and the recession of the 1920s reduced disposable incomes. Moreover, big calibre bolt action rifles cost a lot less than double rifles, and provided the shot was placed accurately were just as effective. Telescopic sights became popular for the smaller bore bolt action rifles but they did not catch on with the shooters of double rifles. The telescope added weight and was slow to use, and the change in balance of 'scope-equipped doubles also badly affected their handling. The introduction of the single trigger was also regarded as a backward step by the seasoned hunter who preferred double triggers. Above all else, a dangerous game rifle has to be reliable, and there is nothing more reliable than a double rifle, each barrel having its own independent lockwork and trigger. On many sets of double triggers, the front one is hinged so it will not bruise the trigger finger during recoil when the second barrel is fired.

ABOVE
Combination guns were frowned upon in England, but are popular in continental Europe, especially with 'superposed' barrels, one above the other.

In many respects the double rifle had reached the peak of its development just prior to World War I. Indeed, the firearms produced today by Holland & Holland, Rigby and Westley Richards would be instantly recognizable to a hunter setting out for the Cape in 1900. The main change to the big bore game rifle since then is principally cosmetic, with the degree and complexity of the engraving changing as personal tastes have altered. Today a best grade, quality double rifle costs from £20,000 ($40,000) upwards and will take up to three years to make. High quality gold inlaid engraving will increase its price, and rifles are now being ordered as works of art rather than tools for killing. One of the world's leading 'virtuoso' engravers is Ken Hunt, who has a three-year waiting list for his work. Some of his creations can be seen in this chapter.

REGULATION

Much of the cost in the manufacture of a double rifle is incurred in the regulation of the barrels. In order to give both barrels the same point of impact at a given distance, they have to be assembled on the action and stock to be test-fired. A wedge between the barrels at the muzzle is tapped in and adjusted until the fall of shot is the same for each barrel. It can be a long process, sometimes involving separating the barrels and rejoining them if they cannot be brought in line with wedges. The rifle must then be used with ammunition of the same bullet weight and ballistics as that used during regulation.

PARADOX BARRELS

In the last century it was not uncommon for dual purpose firearms to be made, which would fire shot or bullet. Some had two sets of barrels, one pair smooth for shot, the other rifled for the solid projectile. Dual-purpose Paradox barrels were made under Fosbery's patent which could fire both, since they were smooth for most of their length with a rifled choke for the last few inches of barrel. Of the Paradox, W W Greener wrote: 'They have the accuracy and force of the heavy rifle combined with the lightness and handiness of a shotgun. Firing black powder and a conical bullet at 100 yards, diagrams measuring about 4 inches by 3 can be obtained. Muzzle velocity of the 12-bore varies from 1050 to 1200 feet per second, with a striking energy at 100 yards of 1722 to 1822 ft lbs according to load and bullet used.'

COMBINATION GUNS

Combination guns were made by English gunmakers in the last century. They consisted of an action with one rifle barrel and one shotgun barrel fitted alongside each other. They gave a hunter the option of a rifle's single-shot power and accuracy for boar or deer, or the shotgun's pellet pattern for wing shooting. Despite these benefits the combination gun was frowned upon in England since it suggested that the owner could not afford both a rifle and a shotgun! In any event the combination did not perform as well as the dedicated firearms, having a worse balance than a shotgun, but more recoil than a rifle. In continental Europe, where there is very restricted ownership of firearms, combination guns which have a rifle barrel under a shotgun tube are still very much in demand. Spanish, German and Italian gunmakers continue to produce combination pieces with a rifle bore of up to 9.3 mm.

BOTTOM LEFT
Most double rifle calibres existed before World War I with the exception of Holland & Holland's 700 NE which was made in 1989. Just a few double rifle Nitro Express cartridges are shown, with a .308 Winchester bolt action rifle cartridge for comparison. From the left: .308 Win, 450 NE, 500-465 NE, 470 NE, 500 NE, 577 NE, 600 NE, 700 NE.

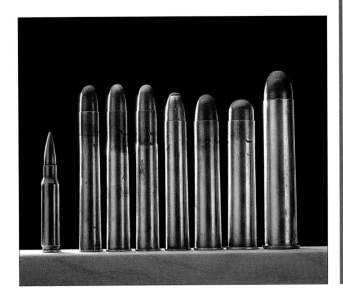

ABOVE
The two leading British manufacturers of sidelock double rifles, Holland & Holland and Rigby, both have distinctive appearances to their actions.

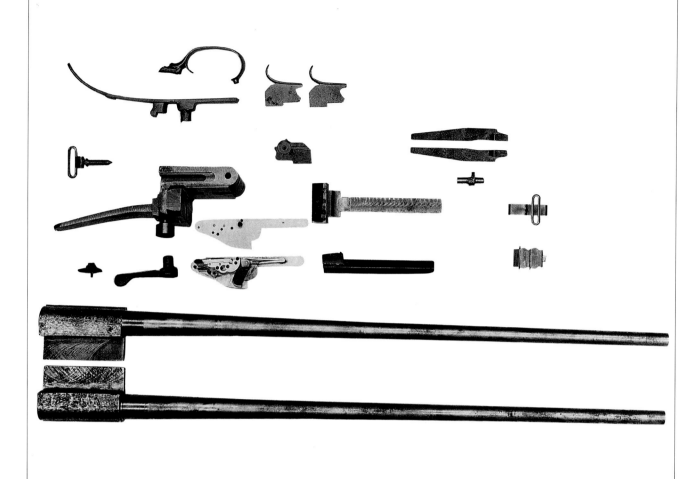

IMMENSE 4-BORES

The first double-barrelled big game guns were smooth-bored percussion pieces of immense size, with barrel diameters of 1.052" (26.7mm) for 4-bores, .835" (21.2 mm) for 8-bores and .775" (19.7 mm) for 10-bores. The bore scale was derived from the number of round lead balls of the bore diameter that would weigh 1 lb. A 4-bore ball would there-fore weigh ¼ lb (113.4 g); an 8-bore ⅛ lb (56.7 g); and a 10-bore 1/10 lb (43.7 g). Even after the invention of the metallic breech-loading cartridge the big bore rifles were still popular because of their increased potency. Bullet weights were as heavy as 1882 grains (122 g) in 4-bores, leaving the muzzle at 1450 fps (442 mps) with an energy of 8832 ft lbs (11,968 joules). The 8-bore proved to be a favou-rite cartridge for thick-skinned dangerous game because it had better penetration than the 4-bore, more muzzle energy than the 10-bore, and a flatter trajectory than both.

EXPRESS RIFLES

As the quality of black powder propellant improved towards the middle of the 19th century, so the calibres of hunting rifles were reduced and the velocity of the bullet increased, creating the description 'Express'. The name was a shorten-ing of 'Express Train' a marketing tag used in 1856 by Purdey for his percussion rifles made for South Africa. These were renowned for their long 'point blank' range, or flat trajectory,

in that virtually the same aim could be taken at 100 yd (91 m) and at 25 yd (23 m) with minimal difference in the point of impact. Compared to the modern high velocity small calibre rifle the trajectory of the Express had a curvature like a rain-bow, but at the time it was considered a substantial improve-ment for the open African plains. The term 'Express' was retained for high velocity, breech-loading, cartridge firing rifles. For some years the .577 Express 2¾" cartridge loaded with black powder was regarded as a fine calibre for big game hunting. The bullet weight of between 500 and 700 grains (32.4 & 45.4 g) delivered up to 4700 ft lbs (6369 joules) of energy at the muzzle, and a striking energy of approximately 3500 ft lbs (4743 joules) at 100 yards. When smokeless propellants became commonplace in the 1890s the .577 case was lengthened to 3" (76.2mm)) and loaded with 100 grains (6.5 g) of cordite behind a 750 grain (48.6 g) bullet. The performance of the new .577 Nitro Express cart-ridge was much improved with a muzzle velocity up to 2050 fps (625 mps) giving a muzzle energy of 7000 ft lbs (9485 joules) and a striking energy at 100 yards of 5680 ft lbs (7697 joules). While this would flatten an elephant quite satisfactorily, it was regarded as overkill for other quarry and a range of other calibres was devised. It was quite common for hunters to have a selection of varying bore rifles at their disposal. From 1880 to 1910 the range of big bore cartridges for double rifles mushroomed and they were available in a variety of high performance calibres.

ABOVE
There have been few changes to the basic design of double rifles since the turn of the century, other than the increasing complexity of the engraving.

.600 NITRO EXPRESS

The .600 Nitro Express was introduced by Jeffrey in 1903 and at one time was regarded as the most powerful commercial cartridge in the world. The 900 grain (58.3 g) bullet powered by 110 grains (7.1 g) of cordite left a double rifle's barrel at 1950 fps (595 mps) with a muzzle energy of 7600 ft lbs (10,298 joules). This level of power has now been exceeded by a number of cartridges designed for bolt-action rifles which started producing very impressive ballistics with smokeless powders at the beginning of this century.

HOLLAND & HOLLAND AND THE .700 EXPRESS

The new .700 Express cartridge is designed for a new double rifle produced by Holland & Holland and is now the most powerful big game cartridge available. The story behind the .700 Express began in 1974 when Holland & Holland ended production of .600 Nitro Express double rifles. They believed that the demand for such large calibres was at an end, and with great fanfare announced the sale of 'The Last H&H .600 Express'. During the 1980s Holland & Holland were asked to build another .600 Express by Mr William Feldstein of Beverly Hills, California. They refused, because they had made a commitment to the purchaser of the previous .600 rifle that his would be their last, and unless he sold it back to them they would not make any more. Feldstein then discussed the problem with Jim Bell of Bell Basic Brass, a speciality cartridge case manufacturer. They came up with the idea of an even bigger cartridge than .600, and Holland & Holland agreed to build rifles in .700 Nitro Express. The first rifle was completed in 1989 and weighed 19 lbs. The original cartridges fired a 1000 grain bullet propelled by 215 grains (13.9 g) of IMR 4831 powder to a velocity of 2020 fps (616 mps) and a muzzle energy of 9050 ft lbs (12,263 joules). The gun is heavy but the well-balanced weight ensures that the recoil is not excessive – just over 136 ft lbs (184 joules) – less than that of some 19th-century 4-bores.

The .700 is not the only double rifle made by Holland & Holland; they will build a rifle to order in virtually any standard calibre specified by the customer. Each rifle is handmade and produced to an exact specification, the size of the action and overall weight being matched to the calibre. The method of construction is similar to that of a double-barrelled side-by-side shotgun, but the action strength is improved to cope with the rifle's higher pressures. The double bite in the receiver, which holds the action closed during firing is supplemented by an additional 'hidden' bite between the ejectors which engages in the breech-face. A rounded thickening of the action known as the bolster (just below the chambers) adds rigidity, and the hammer springs are reversed in the back-action, sidelock trigger group to eliminate the need to remove metal in highly stressed areas.

RIGBY

Another famous London gunmaking company is John Rigby & Co, originally established in Dublin in 1735. A London branch of the company was established in 1865 and the Dublin premises were subsequently closed just prior to the turn of the century. The company was acquired in 1984 by Paul Roberts, a leading London manufacturer of high quality sporting shotguns. Much of Rigby's current production is bolt-action sporting rifles, but they still produce double rifles as well as their sidelock side-by-side shotguns. Like Holland & Holland the rifle actions are much stronger than those of shotguns, but unlike Holland & Holland they still produce .600 Express rifles to order. In addition to the traditional .600 and .577 Nitro Express double rifle calibres, Rigby will chamber their doubles for high performance bolt action rifle cartridges such as .416 Rigby and .458 Win Mag. For a good gunmaker there are almost no limits to what can be built if you have the money and are prepared to wait. Rigby are currently producing for one customer a .775" (10-bore) rifle reminiscent of the Victorian elephant doubles with a spare set of shotgun barrels. The smokeless 10-bore rifle cartridges used will fire a 1100 grain (71.3 g) bullet at 1500 fps (457 mps) for a muzzle energy of 5497 ft lbs (7449 joules). The TKO factor of the three aforementioned biggest double rifle cartridges is: .600 NE – 150; 10-bore – 182; .700 NE – 202. These are all considerably higher than can be achieved with a sporting magazine rifle.

WESTLEY RICHARDS AND THE GORILLA GUN

London is not the only British gunmaking centre producing double rifles. Westley Richards was founded in Birmingham in 1812 for the production of shotguns, rifles and pistols. In 1855 Westley Richards patented and produced the first breech-loading rifle to be used by the British Army. Today, they produce fine sidelock and boxlock shotguns along with boxlock double rifles. The Westley Richards rifles have a most rugged triple bite boxlock action with a characteristic 'dolls head' bite and top lever. The lockwork itself is detachable without tools for easy cleaning and maintenance, a system they first introduced in 1897. The standard calibres offered by the company are: .300 H&H Mag; .375 H&H Mag; .470 Nitro Express; .577 Nitro Express, and .600 Nitro Express, although they will chamber any calibre the customer requires. A recently completed commission for Westley Richards was the .600 NE Gorilla Gun ordered by a wildlife observer and admirer of gorillas. The rifle will probably never be shot by its owner, certainly not an any animal; along with its inlaid case and engraving by Alan Brown and his brother, it is purely an artistic celebration of the gorilla.

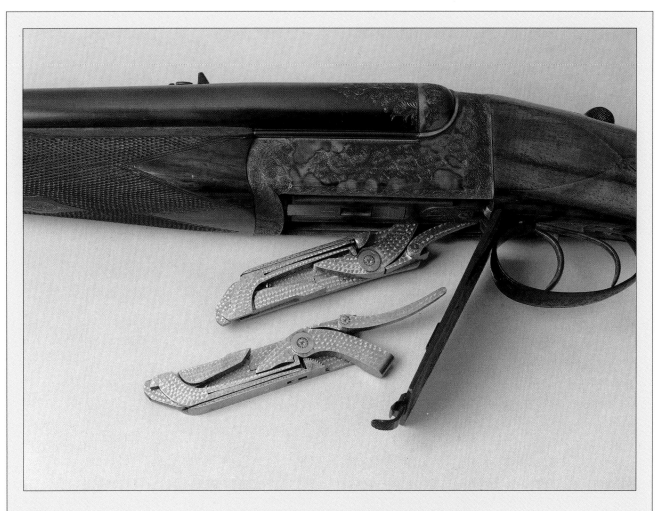

ABOVE
Westley Richard's detail on double
rifles extends to the combination
foresight with folding night sight
and hinged sight protector.

TOP
Westley Richard double rifles have
unique detachable locks.

THIS PAGE
The .600 NE Gorilla Gun (here pictured from a number of different viewpoints) was commissioned from Westley Richards. The ornate engraving on the action and butt plate all feature subtly different aspects of the gorilla's family group and habitat. Despite its decorative nature, the .600 Nitro Express was the most powerful of the big game cartridges produced at the turn of the century.

ITALIAN DOUBLE-BARRELLED RIFLES

ANATOLI ZOLI

In Gardone, the gunmaking region of Italy, Anatoli Zoli produce the Savana range of boxlock, double bite, and double-barrelled rifles. The calibres offered are of only moderate power in big game terms; 9.3mm × 73R; 7mm × 73R and .30–06 Springfield.

RIGHT
Heavy barrels are a feature of all double rifles that are chambered for high pressure big game ammunition.

BELOW
Zoli's side-by-side and over-under double rifles are only chambered for moderate power bolt-action rifle calibres.

ABOVE
The Zoli boxlock actions are not strong enough to be chambered for the most powerful cartridges.

ABOVE AND BELOW
Beretta's SS06 (top) and SS06EEL
over-under rifles will cope with the
higher powered .375 Holland &
Holland and .458 Winchester
Magnum cartridges.

OPPOSITE
The top of Beretta's range is their
side-by-side Model 445 EEL,
featuring ornate silverwork and
beautiful engravings of the big
game hunter's quarry — lions,
leopards, water buffalo and
elephant.

BELOW
The Beretta double rifles made in
Gardone, Italy, are built in the
same way as the classic English big
game rifles.

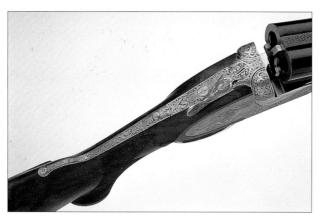

BERETTA

Also in Gardone is Italy's largest and most famous gun company, Pietro Beretta, renowned the world over for their pistols and range of shotguns. Unlike British gunmakers, Beretta make 'over-and-under' or 'superposed' shotguns that have one barrel above the other rather than side-by-side as in classic English game guns. Beretta make a range of double rifles too, both over-and-under and side-by-side models. Like Anatoli Zoli, a lightweight boxlock action is used for their S689 over-and-under rifle, which can also take interchangeable 20-bore shotgun barrels. The S689 is chambered for 9.3mm × 73R and .30–06.

The premium grade Beretta over-and-under sidelock action is used for the SS06 and SS06EEL Express rifles, which are chambered for the higher powered .375 H&H Magnum and .458 Winchester Magnum cartridges. At the top of Beretta's range is their sidelock Model 455 side-by-side express rifle. Made for higher powered ammunition than the over-and-unders, the 455 has an extended forged receiver made from high strength steel to take the high pressures of the rifle cartridges. The standard calibres offered are: .375 H&H Mag, .458 Win Mag, .470 Nitro Express, .500 Nitro Express, and .416 Rigby. The engraving on the Beretta Model 455 is also superb.

HIGH-POWERED
MILITARY RIFLES

RMIES HAVE ALWAYS BEEN THE PRINCIPAL USERS OF FIREARMS and military needs have provided much of the impetus for their development and refinement. Since the 15th century, the rifle and its forbears were virtually the only easily portable weapon at the battle planner's disposal, and they were most effective in the days before vehicles and armour plating. During the 19th century the flintlock rifle gave way first to percussion longarms in the 1830s and then subsequently to breech-loading, metallic cartridge firing carbines and rifles in the 1860s. The breech-loaders had the advantage of higher rates of fire, and the benefit of being reloadable from any position, prone or kneeling. A muzzle-loading flintlock or percussion rifle can only be recharged when standing because of the need to pour the propellant down the barrel into the breech.

BELOW
The French Lebel 8mm (top) was the first 'small bore' bolt military rifle to use smokeless powder and a jacketed bullet in 1886. By 1898 Britain had adopted the similar .303 cartridge which served it through two world wars. The No. 4 rifle (bottom) in .303 was the main British service rifle during and after the Second World War until it was replaced by the FN self-loading rifle chambered for 7.62mm NATO.

The unrest throughout the world in the second half of the 19th century fuelled the desire for new and improved personal weapons, but black powder propellant always proved to be the limiting factor. Apart from the caustic residues left after firing black powder cartridges, the propellant was not capable of the rapid controlled burning needed for high velocity small calibre rounds. In order to gain more power from a black powder weapon therefore, you simply used a bigger bullet and more powder to move it. While this method gave quite high muzzle energies, the velocities were low and trajectories very curved, limiting range and accuracy. The British service rifle cartridge adopted in 1867 was .577 Snider, which used a .750" (14.5mm) diameter 480 grain (31.1 g) bullet travelling at approximately 1250 fps (381 mps) giving a muzzle engery of 1670 ft lbs (2263 joules). This was replaced in 1871 by .577 × .450 Martini-Henry, essentially a .577 case necked down to .450" (11.4mm) using the same weight bullet. The bottlenecked case and smaller bore gave higher velocities and energies – 1350 fps (411 mps) and 1940 ft lbs (2629 joules).

8mm LEBEL 1886

In 1886 the French Army adopted the tubular magazine, bolt-action 8mm Lebel rifle and cartridge, the first 'small bore' military cartridge to use smokeless powder and a

jacketed bullet. This was a considerable advance as both rifles and ammunition were much lighter, and easier for the infantryman to carry than in the previous generation. In addition the tubular magazine permitted a high rate of fire. The 8mm Lebel cartridge itself fired a 198 grain (12.8 g) bullet at 2380 fps (726 mps) giving an energy of 2480 ft lbs (3360 joules). It was not long before other countries started using similar rifles and ammunition.

.303 BRITISH

The United Kingdom adopted the .303 British calibre in 1888, the same year that Germany started using 8mm Mauser. .303 British was loaded with black powder until 1892, after which time the smokeless propellant, Cordite, was used. The cartridge was the British service round until the 1950s when it was replaced by 7.62 mm NATO (.308 Winchester). .303 British was used in Pattern 14 and Lee-Enfield rifles during the First World War, and also in No 4 rifles. The original loading had a 215 grain (13.9 g) bullet travelling at 2180 fps (664 mps) with an energy of 2270 ft lbs (3076 joules). At the time of its replacement the service issue Mk7 .303 British loading had a 174 grain (11.3 g) bullet with a velocity of 2440 fps (743 mps) and an energy of 2300 ft lbs (3118 joules).

.30–06 SPRINGFIELD

In 1892 the USA adopted .30–40 Krag as its first .30 calibre military cartridge, and used it in the bolt action Krag-Jorgensen rifle until 1903 when it was replaced by the Model 1903 Springfield. The cartridge used for the M1903 was also .30" (7.62mm) calibre and fired a 220 grain (14.3 g) round-nosed bullet at 2300 fps (701 mps). Cartridge developments in Europe were tending towards lighter bullets of the same calibre at higher velocities, and the rimless M1903 cartridge was modified in 1906 to use a 150 grain (9.7 g) bullet travelling at 2700 fps (823 mps). The designation of the round was eventually shortened to .30–06 Springfield and became the adopted US military cartridge in various versions until it too was superseded by 7.62mm NATO in the

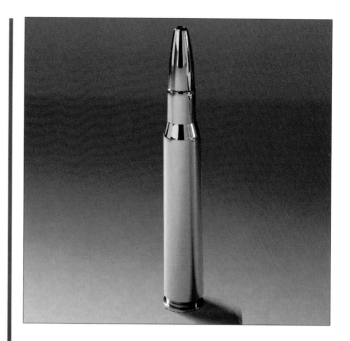

1950s. The .30–06 150 grain bullet was dropped in 1926 in favour of a heavier 172 grain (11.1 g) design at the same velocity given the designation '.30 M1'. This was quite a powerful round producing 2790 ft lbs (3781 joules) of energy.

M1 GARAND

In 1940 the lighter bullet was re-introduced for rifles in the '.30 M2' .30–06 cartridge since the USA had started using a new military self-loading rifle in 1939. The M1 Garand did not work as well with the 172-grain bullet. The heavier .30 M1 load was retained for machine-guns giving a maximum

ABOVE
The US Army used the .30-06 Springfield cartridge from 1906 until it too was replaced by 7.62mm NATO. .30-06 is still a favoured cartridge for bolt action hunting rifles.

BELOW
Springfield Armory's M1A rifle is a semi-automatic version of the M14 service rifle.

ABOVE
The M14/M1A is still in use by
target shooters for their High
Power rifle match.

range of almost 6000 yards, compared to below 4000 with the lighter .30 M2 bullet.

The gas-operated Garand rifle was an important milestone in the development of military smallarms. It was the first self-loading rifle to be issued in quantity to any army and it used an 8-round clip loaded into the integral magazine through the breech. When the clip was emptied it was ejected up through the breech. The breech-bolt rotated along tracks to lock it in to the receiver, and was opened by pressure from a piston that took a gas bleed off from the barrel.

M14

The design was updated in 1957 when the M14 self-loading rifle in 7.62mm NATO was adopted. This used a similar gas-operated self-loading action to the Garand but .had a detachable 20-round box magazine and a selector switch to permit fully automatic fire. The M14 was superseded by the 5.56mm NATO (.223 Remington) M16/AR15 as a general issue rifle in 1967, but remained in service for a considerable time afterwards as a sniping rifle.

At the start of the 20th century virtually all the world's major armies had .284"–.318" (7mm–8mm) calibre bolt action rifles. Attempts to reduce the calibre further at that time did not meet with much success. A .30" (7.62mm) bullet of 150–170 grains (9.7–11.0 g) with a muzzle velocity of between 2300 and 2700 fps (701–823 mps) had what appeared to be the optimum balance of power, accuracy and reliability in theatres of war where the foot soldier fired at ranges of 600 yards or more and the targets were men and horses. Both World Wars were fought with the same basic types of rifle ammunition, the concept of lower powered automatic assault rifles only being introduced by the German and Soviet forces later in World War II.

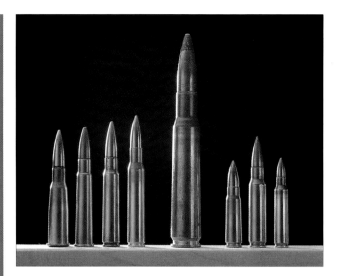

A B O V E
The four cartridges on the left were the main infantry calibres of the First World War: 8mm Lebel, .303 British, 8mm Mauser and .30-06 Springfield. The large cartridge fourth right is .50 Browning developed as a heavy machine-gun and anti-tank round after World War I. It is followed by the Soviet 7.62×39 cartridge, 7.62mm NATO and the latest Western service cartridge, 5.56mm NATO.

B E L O W
7.62×39mm ammunition originally designed for the Soviet SKS carbine is now being used in Western sporting rifles like Ruger's Mini Thirty.

MKb42 AND 7.92 × 33mm

The USSR soon recognized the potential of the 'Sturm-gewehr' or self-loading assault rifles made by Germany in 1942, which fired an intermediate powered cartridge, half-way between pistol calibre submachine-guns and the conventional infantry rifle. The 7.92 × 33mm (7.92 Kurz) ammunition used in the German MKb42 was, in effect, a shorter version of the 7.92 × 57mm (8mm Mauser) rifle cartridge which fires a light 125 grain (7.9 g) bullet at 2250 fps (686 mps).

SKS CARBINE AND 7.62 × 39mm

In 1943 the Soviets began to manufacture their own medium power cartridge, 7.62 × 39mm, which they used in the heavy SKS, a charger loaded, gas-operated, self-loading carbine. The SKS had an integral magazine like the American Garand. It also loaded through the open breech, but from a 10-round charger.

KALASHNIKOV AK47

After the war the Soviets introduced the Avtomat Kalashni-kova, more usually known as the Kalashnikov or AK47, after the year of its design. This too fired the 7.62 × 39mm cart-ridge, which was of similar power to the German 7.92 Kurz round, propelling a 122 grain (7.9 g) bullet to 2330 fps (710 mps) for an energy of 1470 ft lbs (1992 joules). The AK47 was a simple and reliable short-range gas-operated weapon with a box magazine capable of controllable fully automatic fire if required. Along with its successor, the AKM,

the AK47 has been produced in vast quantities (estimated at over 20 million) by the Eastern Bloc and has seen service in virtually every communist-backed conflict since their introduction 44 years ago.

Despite its popularity, the AK47 and its ammunition cannot really be described as powerful. It does not compare with the 'full size' .30" cartridge firing rifles in terms of muzzle velocity and energy, but it does overshadow them in terms of 'firepower', a term frequently used to describe ammunition capacity and cyclic rate without terminal ballistics. There is no doubt that 7.62 × 39mm is effective in skirmishes at short ranges (from 100–250 yards), and this has shaped military thinking in recent years.

7.62mm NATO

The North Atlantic Treaty Organisation (NATO) is a military grouping of Western nations established after World War II to counter what they believed was an expansionist threat from the USSR and the Eastern Bloc. One of their achieve-ments was the standardization of the disparate ammunition used in many Western countries after the two World Wars. During the 1950s most Western nations (including the then West Germany) adopted 7.62mm NATO (7.62mm × 51mm) as their standard rifle cartridge. The round was also marketed as a sporting cartridge by Winchester in the USA as .308

BELOW
Modern military theory prefers 5.56mm smallarms for infantry, of which the Steyr AUG is a good example.

Winchester. The 7.62mm NATO cartridge consolidated the experience of the previous half century, firing a .30" (7.62mm) diameter 150 grain (9.7 g) jacketed bullet at 2750 fps (838 mps) in the US M59 loading; and a 144 grain (9.3 g) bullet at 2700 fps (823 mps) in the British L2A2 Ball loading, giving 2520 and 2330 ft lbs (3415 & 3157 joules) of energy respectively. It proved to be an excellent cartridge, with good accuracy out to 600 yd (549 m) and an effective range from a rifle of over 1000 yd (914 m), easily penetrating the fabric of buildings and unarmoured vehicles at shorter ranges. The 7.62mm NATO cartridge was also suitable for box magazine and belt fed machine-guns and in an emergency the ammunition could be interchanged between these and the infantry rifles.

FN–FAL

The USA used 7.62mm NATO with great success in the M14 rifle, and the UK, along with a dozen other countries, adopted it with Fabrique Nationale's Fusil Automatique Léger (FN–FAL). Like the M14 the FAL had a 20-round box magazine and was gas-operated, although not all models were capable of selective fire. The FAL became known as 'the free world's right arm', being used to fight communist forces in assorted battles from the 1960s to the 1980s.

ABOVE
While 5.56mm has some sniping applications, and some excellent rifles such as the SIG SG 550 use it, the cartridge is limited in range and power.

HECKLER & KOCH G3

Despite developing the moderate powered assault rifle for the Third Reich during World War II, the Germans dropped it afterwards and manufactured a full power rifle to use 7.62 NATO ammunition. The Heckler & Koch G3 was derived from a Spanish CETME design. The G3 used a roller delayed blowback system of self-loading in which the cartridge was locked in the chamber by two rollers and a hollow locking piece that moved slowly as the bullet travelled down the barrel at great velocity during firing. By the time the pressure had dropped in the chamber the locking piece and rollers no longer prevented the bolt from moving back, extracting and ejecting the case, re-cocking the hammer and re-chambering a fresh cartridge.

RISE OF 5.56mm

Regrettably, the 7.62mm NATO has now fallen from favour as the preferred cartridge for individual weapons, though it

ABOVE
7.62mm NATO is preferred for
heavy duty use, and SAM Inc have
produced a dual purpose law
enforcement weapon called the
Crossfire which has two sections,
one for 7.62mm and one of
12 gauge shotshells.

has been retained for sniping and machine-gun use.

The current military view is that infantry will not engage the enemy with hand-held weapons at extended ranges; that function being reserved for vehicle-mounted cannon, heavy machine-guns or artillery. Explosive guided rockets are now employed against vehicles or buildings, and the foot soldier is better equipped with a lightweight weapon firing small calibre ammunition. The result of this in recent years has been the issue of self-loading rifles of 5.56mm (.223") calibre.

The most common NATO rifle calibre used today is 5.56 × 45mm, also sold commercially as .223 Remington. The standard American M193 ball ammunition uses a 55 grain (3.6 g) bullet, which is fired at approximately 3300 fps (1006 mps) from an M16 rifle giving a muzzle energy of 1339 ft lbs (1814 joules). While 5.56mm is extremely accurate and has a very flat trajectory at short ranges coupled with low recoil when firing, the light bullet slows down very rapidly, and is easily blown off course in a strong wind. At 300 yd (274 m) the velocity has fallen to 2000 fps (610 mps) and the energy has dropped to 490 ft lbs (664 joules). At 600 yd (549 m) the velocity is only 1150 fps (351 mps) and the energy is down to 160 ft lbs (217 joules). By comparison the 7.62mm NATO cartridge with a 150 grain (9.7 g) bullet still has 1500 ft lbs (2033 joules) of energy at 300 yards and just under 1000 ft

lbs (1355 joules) at 600 yards. British marines discovered the shortcomings of the 5.56mm cartridge during the Falklands War when they were hitting their enemy at 600 yards but were not preventing them from fighting back. It has been callously observed that the current popularity of the 5.56mm cartridge is due to the fact that it will wound more than it will kill. A wound is preferable to a kill, not for reasons of compassion but because a wounded soldier uses up more of the enemy's resources than a dead one; he will need to be moved back from the front line to a field hospital rather than just buried on the battlefield.

7.62mm NATO FOR SNIPING

It is no surprise that the powerful 7.62mm NATO cartridge has been retained by many NATO countries for use in sniping weapons, and that a large number of the rifles are in fact bolt action rather than self-loading. Bolt-action rifles are lighter than their self-loading counterparts in the same cali-bre and are generally far more accurate, being made to far higher tolerances. One exception to this is the Heckler & Koch PSG1 high precision marksman's rifle based on their popular G3 7.62mm NATO self-loading rifle. The manu-facturers claim that a 5-shot group fired at 300 metres will measure no more than 80mm. This is an accuracy of one minute of angle, comparable with many bolt-action rifles, although the best of them can get down to half a minute of angle or less.

OTHER SNIPING CALIBRES

While 7.62mm NATO is still the preferred calibre for Western sniping rifles, the widespread adoption of 5.56mm for general infantry use has reduced the need for snipers to use issue ammunition. The 7.62mm sniping rounds tend to have heavier bullets up around 180–185 grains (11.7–12.0 g) weight, and in England and the USA other calibres are being used because they have higher energy than 7.62mm NATO and a flatter trajectory at extended ranges. In addition to 7.62mm NATO, Accuracy International of Portsmouth, UK, currently chamber their bolt PM (L96A1) sniper rifle for 7mm Remington Magnum and .300 Winchester Magnum, which can be used at ranges of up to 1000 yards. Armalon in London also produce their BGR sniper rifle with a rigid ribbed barrel in the same calibres.

ABOVE
For long range sniping, 7.62mm NATO has been retained, and Parker Hale's bolt action M85 rifle has been adopted by a number of armies.

FACING PAGE, RIGHT
Mauser's bolt action Model 86SR sniper rifles are available with laminated (left) or synthetic stocks (right).

BELOW
The SIG-Sauer SSG2000 Precision sniping rifle is based on the proven bolt action of the Sauer 80/90 rifles.

.338 SUPER MAGNUM

A dedicated version of Accuracy's PM in a new calibre has also been made for even longer range sniping. The .338 Super Magnum rifle fires a 250 grain (16.2 g) bullet at 3000 fps (914 mps) with a muzzle energy of almost 5000 ft lbs (6775 joules). The bullet is still supersonic at 1500 yards (1400 metres) and has 740 ft lbs of energy (1000 joules). At the time of writing, however, this ammunition was only being produced by Lapua in Finland. The ballistics of the cartridge are very similar to those of .338 BELL, and the dimensions identical. The .338 BELL was an experimental .338 cartridge based on the .416 Rigby case and made in 1983 by Brass Extrusion Laboratories Ltd in Illinois for US Navy tests.

BELOW
Accuracy's PM (L96A1) rifle is chambered for the standard 7.62 NATO round as well as for 7mm Rem Magnum and .300 Winchester Magnum, both of which have flatter trajectories.

RIGHT
.338 Lapua Magnum cartridges.

THE TANK BUSTERS

Tanks first appeared during the Western Front battles of the First World War. They began as moderately armoured gun platforms capable of crossing No-Man's-Land between opposing forces giving a measure of protection to their crew. As the war progressed the armour was made thicker so that it could not be penetrated by steel cored ammunition fired from conventional rifles. Between the wars there was rapid development of anti-tank rifles and ammunition, designed to penetrate the moderate levels of armour that were then being developed.

TANK-GEWEHR M1918

The first successful design was the Mauser Tank-Gewehr Modell 1918, which was little more than an overgrown Mauser '98 action with a large calibre, long heavy barrel, bipod and heavy wooden stock. The M1918 fired a 13mm steel cored 965 grain (62.5 g) bullet at approximately 3000 fps (913 mps). The very high muzzle energy generated, 19,280 ft lbs (26,125 joules), was sufficient to penetrate ¾" (19mm) of armour plate at 110 yards (100 metres). The high recoil generated by the powerful 13 × 92mm SR round was absorbed by the heavy rifle.

7.92 PANZERBÜCHSE

By 1938, the German Army had refined their anti-tank rifle to use a necked down and derimmed derivative of the 13 × 92mm SR Tank-Gewehr case. The new cartridge, 7.92 × 94mm or 7.92mm Panzerbüchse, fired a 222 grain (14.4 g) bullet with an armour piercing tungsten carbide core and a tear gas capsule at a velocity of 3975 fps (1210 mps) with an energy of around 7800 ft lbs (10,569 joules). The idea was that the bullet would pierce the vehicle armour and then release the tear gas causing the crew to abandon the vehicle. While penetration of armour over an inch thick (26mm) was achieved there are no known incidences of the tear gas actually being released. The weapon used to fire the cartridge was known as the Panzerbüchse Modell 38 and was another single-shot rifle of 35 lb weight (15.9 kg). Unlike the bolt-action Mauser M1918 design, the M38 had a recoiling barrel assembly that opened the breech by a cam on its return to battery. The design proved too expensive to manufacture in great numbers and a simplified manually operated version was made in 1939 to fire the same cartridge. In any case, by the time the Modell 39 was operational, tank armour had become sufficiently impenetrable.

7.92mm WZ 35

During 1935 the Polish Army took delivery of their own 7.92mm calibre anti-tank rifle, which also used a tungsten-cored bullet fired from an oversized case. Similar to the German Mauser M1918, the wz 35 was based on a strong repeating bolt action with bipod and wooden stock. To increase portability the wz 35 was stripped of all unnecessary furniture and the weight reduced to 20 lb (9.1 kg). Recoil was reduced by the use of a muzzle brake on the end of the barrel. The muzzle velocity was very high, at 4200 fps (1280 mps), although the barrel 'wore' after 200 rounds had been fired. After that it dropped to around 3800 fps (1158 mps) with a rapid decrease in penetration. Before Poland was overrun by Germany their weapons engineers had been working on a Gerlich-type squeeze bore rifle with a tapered barrel starting at 11mm (.45") at the breech, and reducing to 7.92mm (.318") at the muzzle. The bullet had a tungsten core with a lead sleeve and a jacket with deformable driving band, which reduced during the trip up the barrel. The velocity claimed for the projectile was almost 5000 fps (1540 mps) and would have had significant penetrating power had it ever gone into production.

.55 BOYS

Named after one of its principal designers, the .55 Boys was the British anti-tank rifle and cartridge adopted in 1937. A 36 lb (16.3 kg) bolt-action repeating rifle with a vertical top mounted 5-round magazine, the Boys used a belted cartridge similar in appearance to those of high performance sporting rifles – apart from the size and power. Mk1 ammunition for the Boys had a 926 grain (60 g) bullet and the Mk2 a lighter 735 grain (48 g) bullet that reached approximately 2900 fps (884 mps) with an energy of 13,722 ft lbs (18,594 joules). The Boys rifle could penetrate ¾" (19mm) of armour at 300 yards (275 m).

ABOVE

The comparative lightness of the .55 Boys rifle meant that it could be easily moved by one man. Surviving examples of this short-lived anti-tank rifle are popular with American and British target shooters and military re-enactment groups.

The Finnish 20mm Lahti anti-tank rifle of 1939 was derived from Lahti's aircraft cannon with only minor modification. The gas-operated self-loading rifle fed ammunition from a 10-round box magazine which clipped into the top of the breech. A masterpiece of engineering, the 95 lb (43 kg) Lahti had a rack and pinion rotary cocking handle, a rotating muzzle brake and a twin bipod. One set of bipod legs had conventional spiked feet, the other had small skis to allow the rifle to be pushed forwards on snow for better aim. The Lahti was about as large a rifle as one man could manage, and then only with difficulty. Only 1906 of the L39 were produced. When it was first made, the ammunition could penetrate the armour of Russian T26 tanks, but proved ineffective against the tougher T34. Reports of both the bullet weight and muzzle velocity have varied, but one recently verified source has put the weight of the solid tungsten bullet at 2,310 grains (149.7 g) and the velocity at 2700 to 2800 fps (823–853 mps). Even at the lower velocity this is a muzzle energy of 37,400 ft lbs (50,678 joules), almost three times that of the .55 Boys, making the Lahti one of the most powerful one-man rifles ever made.

TOP LEFT
A rotary cocking handle is used to cock the bolt.

TOP RIGHT
Skids were fitted to allow the Lahti to be pushed forwards over snow for a better aim.

ABOVE
The Lahti's breech block and ammunition are both immense.

OVERLEAF
The self-loading 20mm Lahti was about as powerful a rifle as could be handled by one man and fired from prone without a vehicle mount.

20mm SOLOTHURN

There were a number of 20mm Solothurn anti-tank rifles. The first was the S-18/100 made in 1934 that fired the 20 × 105B or 20mm Short Solothurn cartridge. The S-18/100 was a recoil operated semi-automaic repeater using a side-entry 5- or 10-round magazine. The later model S-18/1000 was acquired and modified by the Germans and used as their Panzerbüchse Modell 41 (PzB 41), again with a side-entry box magazine. Like the similarly powered 20mm Lahti, the PzB 41 firing 20mm Solothurn was ineffective against T34 tanks.

.50 BROWNING, BARRETT AND McMILLAN

.50 Browning (.50 BMG) was one of the most enduring cartridges used with anti-tank rifles. Like most of the world's armies, the USA began developing anti-tank and heavy machine-gun ammunition at the end of World War I. The experimental cartridges ranged from .50" up to .80" in bullet diameter. .50 Browning was used in the M1918 Winchester anti-tank rifle but was more commonly found in belt-fed machine-guns. It is still used by many military forces against light armoured vehicles and buildings, being fired from an automatic four barrelled 'Quad 50'. The .50 Browning cartridge has also been used in the resurgence of bolt action and self-loading repeating rifles for sniping, as the trajectory

BELOW
The resurgence of .50 Browning for both sniping and sporting use has created a demand for modern self-loading .50 calibre rifles like the Barrett M82A1.

BELOW AND FACING PAGE
McMillan's bolt action .50 calibre rifles are light in weight at 24 lbs, with recoil reduced by a massive compensator.

of the cartridge is extremely flat out to 600 yards, dropping only a few inches. The manufacturers are exclusively American. Barrett Firearms Manufacturing Inc in Muirfreesboro, Tennessee, USA, produce their Model 82A1 short recoil self-loader with an 11-round detachable box magazine, a 33-inch barrel and an unloaded weight of 32.5 lbs (14.7 kg). A bullpup version with a shorter overall length has also been announced. McMillan & Co of Phoenix, Arizona, produce two bolt-action models, the M87 and M88 in .50 BMG. Both have 29" (737mm) barrels and weigh just over 20 lbs (9.1 kg) without a telescopic sight. From the barrel of the Barrett M82A1, US M33 ball ammunition will drive a 660 grain (42.9 g) bullet to 2800 fps (853 mps) and a muzzle energy of 11,490 ft lbs (15,569 joules) making it the world's most powerful current production rifle.

GLOSSARY

ACP Abbreviation for cartridge designation 'Automatic Colt Pistol'.

ACTION Generalized description of part or all of a firearm's mechanism concerned with loading and/or firing, eg 'bolt action', 'Martini action'.

AE Abbreviation for cartridge designation 'Action Express'.

A-SQUARE Brand name of the A-Square Co. in Madison, Indiana, USA, manufacturers of rifles and ammunition.

AUTO 1) Suffix to cartridge designation indicating that the round is designed for use in self-loading pistols; 2) Shortened form of 'automatic' that is often applied to self-loading pistols. These are generally 'semi-automatic' rather than 'fully automatic'.

AUTOMAG Brand name for high powered self-loading pistols and ammunition originally made during the early 1970s. The name is perpetuated on pistols produced by iAi and AMT in America.

BACK ACTION Trigger mechanism where the lockwork is located behind the breech.

BELLING OUT Part of wildcat cartridge manufacture which increases the diameter of the case mouth to take a larger than standard bullet.

BELTED CASE CARTRIDGE Cartridge with an external strengthening ring at the head.

BELTED MAGNUM Description of high powered rifle ammunition which has an external strengthening ring on the head of the cartridge case.

BLACK POWDER Also known as gunpowder. Black powder is a mixture of 75% potassium nitrate (saltpetre), 15% charcoal and 10% sulphur. The earliest form of reliable propellant known it is still used in antique and replica 'muzzle loading' weapons, but has been superseded by nitrocellulose and nitroglycerine based propellants for modern handguns.

BLOWBACK Operating method of small calibre self-loading pistols. The breech block is held closed by spring pressure which, with the inertia of the breech block, holds the cartridge in the chamber of the barrel on firing. Once inertia is overcome by recoil, the breech moves back freely controlled by the recoil spring, ejecting the fired case and loading a fresh cartridge into the chamber.

BLUEING Otherwise known as 'blacking'. Controlled corrosion of the surface of ferrous steel that results in a thin inert blue/black layer on the surface, offering some protection against further corrosion.

BOLSTER Thickened and rounded area of a double rifle's action used to increase strength.

BOLT ACTION Description of a firearm loading mechanism which uses a manually operated bolt to lock the cartridge in the chamber.

BOTTLENECKED Description of a cartridge which steps down to a smaller diameter from the base of the case to the neck. Usually seen in rifle ammunition, but also used in a few self-loading pistol calibres.

BOXLOCK Trigger mechanism where the locks are contained in a closed box below the breech.

BREAK-TOP Handgun, shotgun or rifle which is loaded or unloaded by unlatching the barrel and chamber/cylinder and swinging it down to open the breech. Typical examples are the Webley revolvers, Thompson/Center Contender pistols and double-barrelled rifles.

BREECH (BREACH) The end of a barrel in which combustion takes place when the weapon is fired.

BREECH-LOADING Description of firearm used with cartridges that are inserted into an open breech to load. The breech is closed with a bolt, slide, falling block or lever to contain pressure during firing.

BROOMHANDLE Nickname given to the Mauser Model C1896 pistol which had a distinctive wooden butt.

BRUSH CARTRIDGE General description of a moderate to high powered cartridge which is used for short range hunting in the USA.

BULLET Shaped projectile fired from a firearm. Generally made from a lead alloy and often covered with a copper or steel coating for use in high velocity ammunition. 'Bullet' does not refer to a complete round of ammunition.

BULLPUP Shortened rifle action which places the magazine behind the trigger rather than in front of it. Though it shortens the overall length of the firearm, it limits the use to firing from only one shoulder.

BURST FIRE Trigger mechanism that permits firing of more than one round of ammunition with each pull of the trigger. Interrupters stop each burst after a preset number of rounds (usually two or three). Burst fire should not be confused with fully automatic fire, which will only stop when the trigger is released or the magazine emptied.

CALIBRE (CALIBER) 1) Measurement of the bore of a firearm made across the lands of the rifling. It is the bore of the barrel after subtracting the depth of the rifling grooves; 2) Name given to cartridge designation of a weapon and ammunition which may or may not be the same as the exact bore of the firearm.

CAM Projection or lug on a barrel or bolt which changes the direction of the component under linear force.

CARTRIDGE Complete round of ammunition comprising case, primer, propellant and bullet.

CENTREFIRE (CENTERFIRE) Cartridges that have a central primer or percussion cap in the need of the cartridge case.

CHAMBER Part of the barrel or cylinder that contains the cartridge on firing.

CYLINDER Major component of a revolver containing chambers that hold the cartridges and brings them in line with the barrel as the hammer/trigger is cocked.

DAGG Name given to early wheel-lock pistols.

DELAYED BLOWBACK Mechanism for preventing the breech block opening in a self-loading weapon until the bullet has left the barrel and the breech pressure has dropped. Most common is the Browning delayed blowback system which keeps the barrel locked into the slide with lugs until the pressure drops, whereupon the barrel cams down and permits the slide to cycle by blowback. The Walther/Beretta wedge delayed blowback system also locks the slide and barrel using a pivoting wedge which is forced down by an internal rod as the slide moves backwards.

DERRINGER   Originally a large bore single-shot pistol sold by Philadelphia gunsmith Henry Deringer. The name has been corrupted to derringer and is most commonly used to describe small 2-shot handguns.

DISCONNECTOR   Internal device in a self-loading weapon that prevents fully automatic fire and necessitates the release of the trigger before firing subsequent shots.

DOUBLE ACTION (DA)   Description of trigger mechanism that can be cocked and fired by pulling the trigger or can be manually cocked by pulling back the hammer which results in a lighter trigger pull. Also applied to the trigger-cocking shooting method.

EXPRESS   1) Shortened form of 'Express Train', a description used for a high velocity Purdey rifle made in 1856. Adopted at the end of the century for high velocity ammunition with a flat trajectory. 2) Description of open sights fitted to big game rifles that are swift to align with the target.

EXTERIOR BALLISTICS   Study of the flight of a projectile through the air after it has left a firearm's barrel.

FALLING BLOCK   Type of breech-loading action using a block of steel which rises vertically to close the chamber.

FBI   Federal Bureau of Investigation, an American law enforcement agency.

FFg   American measurement of grain size of black powder propellant. FFg is large and slow burning, FFFFg is small and fast burning.

FIREPOWER   Term given to combination of cyclic rate or ammunition capacity of a firearm along with the power of individual cartridges.

FLINTLOCK   17th-century firearm ignition system in which a flint clamped in a swinging arm was propelled by spring pressure against a steel. This resulted in a shower of sparks, which ignited fine black powder placed in a 'pan', which in turn ignited the main propellant charge.

FLOBERT   Early rimfire type cartridge design where priming compound covered the entire inside of the cartridge.

FPS   Abbreviation for Feet Per Second, an imperial measurement of velocity.

FULMINATE   Chemical compound which detonates on impact. Mercury Fulminate was used for primers and percussion caps in early firearms. Lead Styphnate is used for modern non-corrosive primers.

GAS CUTTING   Erosion of a firearm by the flame and pressure generated during firing.

GAS OPERATION   Method of cycling a self-loading firearm using the propellant gases to push back the breech.

HANDCANNON   1) Brand name for Thompson/Center Contender pistols which have been converted by SSK Industries to fire exceedingly high powered ammunition for hunting or silhouette shooting; 2) Early hand-held firearm of large bore.

HANDLOAD   Home manufacture of ammunition by a shooter. Handloading is used to tailor the ammunition to the characteristics of the firearm and the use to which it is put. Handloading can increase accuracy and alter the power of the weapon.

HEADSPACE   1) Distance between the base of the cartridge and the face of the breech; 2) Reference point at which the cartridge is located in the chamber. For revolvers this is usually the rim at the base of the cartridge; for self-loading pistols this is often the mouth of the case at the front of the chamber. Bolt action rifles, with bottlenecked rimless ammunition, headspace on the case shoulder.

H&H   Abbreviation of Holland & Holland, a British gun-making company.

HOLLOWPOINT   Bullet design with a hollow nose which is designed to expand and mushroom on impact giving greater shock effect. Sometimes erroneously referred to as 'Dum Dums'.

IPSC   International Practical Shooting Confederation. The international controlling body for one type of action or combat-style target shooting.

KENGIL   Brand name for a British single-shot pistol used for long-range target shooting.

LANDS   Raised area of rifling that bites into the bullet and imparts stabilizing spin.

LEVER ACTION   Breech-loading mechanism using a lever to open the breech, eject the fired cartridge case and insert a fresh round of ammunition.

LOCK   General term for firearm sub-assembly which is involved with holding breech closed and/or effecting firing of the cartridge.

LUGS   Raised areas on barrels or bolts which engage in mating recesses in the slide or breech.

MACHINE PISTOL   Small, fully-automatic firearm that fires a pistol cartridge. Also known as sub-machine guns (SMG), but SMG is also applied to some small fully-automatic firearms that fire moderate and full power rifle cartridges.

MAGNUM   Originally a cartridge suffix used to denote powerful high pressure ammunition or high velocity. Now appears on some new low pressure calibres as a marketing ploy rather than an indication of terminal effectiveness. The original pistol Magnums, .357 and .44 have been overtaken in the power league by the Maximums, Supermags and Casull calibres.

MARS   High-powered pistol designed by Hugh W Gabbet-Fairfax at the turn of the 20th century.

MINOR CALIBRE   Low-scoring band designated by the IPSC for shooters using ammunition where the product of the bullet weight in grains and velocity in feet per second, divided by 1000 is equal to/greater than 125. Originally derived from the momentum of .38 Special revolver ammunition, it is now based on the momentum of a 115 grain 9mm Luger bullet when fired from a 4" barrelled pistol.

MPS Abbreviation of metres per second, a metric measurement of velocity.

MULTI CALIBER Brand name for a conversion to the Colt 1911 pistol by Peters-Stahl in West Germany, which permits different calibre barrels and ammunition to be used with the same frame and slide.

MUZZLE End of the barrel from which the projectile emerges during firing.

MUZZLE ENERGY Energy of a bullet when it leaves a firearm barrel. Calculated in foot-pounds (ft lbs) from the square of the velocity, multiplied by the bullet weight in pounds, divided by twice the acceleration due to gravity. Since the acceleration due to gravity is a constant, the equation can be reduced to $ME = (V^2 \times BW)/450240$. Also measured in joules, which is the muzzle energy in ft lbs multiplied by 1.355, or in kilogram metres, which is the energy in ft lbs multiplied by 0.1383.

MUZZLE LOADING Method of loading weapons with chambers or barrels closed at one end. Propellant is poured down into the chamber and the bullet or ball projectile rammed down on top. Ignition can be by flint, match, wheel, or percussion cap. Muzzle loaders use low pressure black powder or its substitutes rather than modern high pressure products as propellants.

MUZZLE VELOCITY Speed of bullet when it leaves a firearm's barrel. Measured in feet per second (fps) or metres per second (mps).

NATO North Atlantic Treaty Organisation. A military grouping of some Western countries.

NECK DOWN Part of wildcat cartridge manufacture which decreases the diameter of the case mouth to take a smaller than standard bullet.

NIPPLE Hollow stub at the breech end of a muzzle loading firearm on to which a percussion cap is placed. When the hammer falls on the percussion cap it is crushed between the hammer and the nipple, exploding and sending a flame through the nipple to the main powder charge.

NITROCELLULOSE Base material for modern high pressure non-corrosive propellant. Nitrocellulose is mixed with retardants and sometimes nitroglycerine to modify its burning rate and give greater versatility in different weapons.

PEACEMAKER Alternative name for Colt's Single Action Army model revolver first made in 1872.

PEPPERBOX Early 19th-century repeating handguns. In effect they were revolvers without a barrel, each chamber being elongated to form a short integral barrel without rifling. Rendered obsolete by the introduction of Colt's revolver, they were still popular until the American Civil War.

PERCUSSION Name given to the explosive effect of certain salts or detonating compounds when struck. When the salts are contained in a thin copper cup the result is a percussion cap that is placed on a nipple of a black-powder firearm. Modern primers are also a type of percussion cap which form an integral part of a cartridge.

POWER FACTOR Name given to the result of the IPSC Major and Minor calibre calculation.

POWER FLOOR Minimum power level for IPSC major and minor power ratings.

PRIMER Impact sensitive percussion cap used in centrefire ammunition, which is inserted into the centre of the cartridge base. Ignites the main propellant charge when struck.

PROPELLANT Principal consumable component of ammunition. When ignited, propellants burn at a very high rate generating high pressure gas. The gas propels the bullet out of the cartridge case and up the barrel of the firearm.

PYRITE Yellow mineral formed from sulphur and iron that was used to create sparks in wheel-lock ignition.

REAMING Rotary removal of metal to enlarge a hole. Used in wildcat cartridge manufacture to thin down the wall of cartridge cases that have been cut back.

RECIPROCATE Linear movement back and forth. The slide of a pistol reciprocates during firing, as does the breech-block of a self-loading rifle.

REGULATION Adjusting a firearm so that the fall of shot is at the same point at the sights. Often used to describe the adjustment of double-barrelled rifles so that both barrels shoot to the same point of impact.

REVOLVER Handgun type which has a fixed barrel and a revolving cylinder.

RIFLING Helical grooves inside a firearm barrel that impart stabilizing spin to a bullet as it travels down the bore.

RIMFIRE Cartridge type in which the priming compound is located in the thin rim of the cartridge case base. One of the first metallic cartridge types, still popular today for target shooting and pest control.

ROLLER LOCKED Method of creating delayed blowback in self-loading weapons by locking the breech with rollers until the chamber pressure drops.

ROUND Single unit of ammunition also called a cartridge.

SAA Abbreviation for Colt's Single Action Army model revolver first made in 1872.

SALTPETRE (SALTPETER) Common name for chemical compound potassium nitrate (KNO_3), a component of black powder (gunpowder).

SEAR Component of trigger mechanism that holds hammer or striker back prior to firing.

SELF-LOADING Description of an action type which, when fired, automatically ejects the spent case, re-cocks the hammer or striker and chambers a fresh cartridge.

SIDELOCK Firing mechanism where the lock is mounted on plate fitted to the side of the stock.

SINGLE ACTION (SA)   Also known as hammer cocking or thumb cocking in revolvers, where it is necessary to thumb back the hammer in order to index the cylinder and prepare the revolver for firing. Applied to self-loading pistols that cannot be fired by trigger-cocking.

SLIDE   Part of a firearm, usually of a self-loading pistol, which contains the breech block and moves backwards and forwards during firing and chambering a fresh cartridge.

SMALLBORE   General description of firearms that chamber .22″ rimfire ammunition.

SMOKELESS POWDER   Propellant type based on nitro-cellulose, which was introduced at the turn of the 20th century. Produces much less smoke and residue than black powder.

SNAPHAUNCE   Early type of flintlock.

SUPERMAG   Wildcat cartridge family designed by Elgin Gates of the International Metallic Silhouette Shooting Association (IMSSA).

TKO   Taylor Knock Out, a power indicator used by the African hunter, John Taylor. The TKO is calculated by multiplying the bullet diameter in inches by its weight in grains and by the muzzle velocity in feet per second. This figure is then divided by 7000 to arrive at the final TKO factor.

TOGGLE LOCK   Barrel locking system used in Maxim machine-guns, which was adapted by Borchardt and Luger for their self-loading pistols.

TORQUE   Description of the twisting force. Causes rotation under recoil of a firearm.

TRIGGER-COCKING   Method of firing a handgun where pulling the trigger cocks then fires the piece. Incorrectly known as 'double action', as many handguns have been made that can only fire when trigger-cocked and hence are a form of single action.

TRIGGER TRAVEL   Movement of trigger needed before weapon is fired.

UZI   Brand name for Israel Military Industries self-loading pistols and machine-guns, from the original designer's name.

WHEEL-LOCK   First reliable firearm ignition system dating from the 16th century, in which a steel wheel is spun against iron pyrites to create sparks for propellant ignition.

WILDCAT   A cartridge that is not made commercially. Wildcats are produced by altering the shape, size, capacity or calibre of standard cartridge cases.

WIN MAG   Abbreviation for Winchester Magnum used after calibre to describe a cartridge, eg .338 Win Mag.

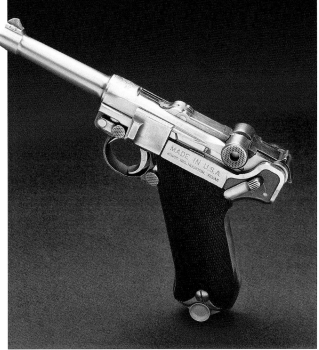

OPPOSITE

Steyr's AUG rifle is compact and light, a feature of the bullpup design.

ABOVE

The Israeli-manufactured Desert Eagle self-loading pistol has been chambered for the revolver calibres .357 Magnum, .41 Magnum and .44 Magnum (illustrated). The latest models are chambered for a new dedicated cartridge: .50 Action Express.

LEFT

The Luger P'08 pistol design from the turn of the century introduced the 9mm Luger cartridge, which is now one of the most popular mid-powered pistol cartridges in the world. In 1991, Mitchell Arms in the US produced the first stainless steel replica of the P'08.

PICTURE CREDITS

Rob Adam: 9, 21t, 36t&b, 37t&b, 58tl, 73, 74t & inset, 110t, 113l&r, 114, 115, 116–17; **Norma:** 10t, 14t, 38t, 81l&r, 104t; **Lapua:** 12b, 111b; **Springfield Armory:** 13, 51, 52, 53t, 63, 64tr, 66, 104b, 105; **Freedom Arms:** 14b, 32b; **John Taffin:** 15, 16b, 32t, 33, 34t&b, 35b, 42t&b, 43; **Thompson/Center Arms:** 17, 67br; **Kimber:** 17b, 71, 77; **Beretta:** 18, 77, 100, 101; **Westley Richards:** 19tl, 89t, 93, 96b, 97t&b, 98; *Combat & Survival magazine:* 20, 112; **McMillan:** 21b, 118t, 119b; **Smith & Wesson:** 23, 28, 38b, 41, 45, 57t; **Sturm, Ruger & Co:** 24, 29, 30b, 46, 80t, 106b; **Colt's Manufacturing Co.:** 30t, 31t, 50, 55; **Frank James:** 35t, 57b; **Matra Manhurin:** 39b; **R. Beel:** 40t; **Wildey:** 47, 61t; **LAR Manufacturing:** 54t; **New Detonics Co:** 54t; **Star:** 56t; **Glock:** 58b; **Walt Rauch:** 60r; **Ultra Light Arms:** 65; **Pachmayr:** 67t&bl; **SSK Industries:** 58; **Mag-Na-Port:** 69t; **Magnum Research:** 69b, 125t; **USRAC:** 72, 82t; **Browning:** 74b, 75t, 77; **Marlin:** 75b; **Musgrave:** 77; **Holland & Holland:** 78t, 94, 95; **Rigby:** 78b, 79t, 91t&br, 92, 96t; **Weatherby:** 82t, 83b, 84; **A-Square:** 85t&b, 86, 87; **A. Zoli:** 99; **Steyr Mannlicher:** 107, 124; **SIG:** 108 110b; **SAM:** 109; **Mauser:** 111t; **Accuracy International:** 111c; **Barrett:** 118t.

ACKNOWLEDGEMENTS

The author would like to thank the following companies and individuals who lent firearms and ammunition for inclusion in the photographs by Paul Forrester: A Baldwin, S Boulter, A Cutler-Andrews, J Fielden, N Green, N Jennings, W Martin, Ranger Firearms, Westley Richards and Wildey Inc.